NEGATION AND THEOLOGY

NEGATION
AND
THEOLOGY

Edited by
ROBERT P. SCHARLEMANN
with Essays and Replies by
DAVID E. KLEMM,
MARK C. TAYLOR,
EDITH WYSCHOGROD,
JANE MARY TRAU,
LANGDON GILKEY,
and MASAO ABE

University Press of Virginia
Charlottesville and London

THE UNIVERSITY PRESS OF VIRGINIA
Copyright © 1992 by the Rector and Visitors
of the University of Virginia

First published 1992

Library of Congress Cataloging-in-Publication Data

Negation and theology : edited by Robert P. Scharlemann ; with essays
and replies by David E. Klemm . . . [et al.].
p. cm. — (Studies in religion and culture)
Includes bibliographical references.
ISBN 0-8139-1380-2
1. Nothing (Philosophy)—History—20th century.   2. God—History
of doctrines—20th century.   3. Philosophy and religion—
History—20th century.   4. Derrida, Jacques.   5. Tillich, Paul,
1886–1965.   I. Scharlemann, Robert P.   II. Klemm, David E., 1947–   .
III. Series : Studies in religion and culture (Charlottesville, Va.)
BD398.N44   1922
291.2—dc20   91–46593
                                                                                        CIP

Printed in the United States of America

CONTENTS

1.   Introduction
        ROBERT P. SCHARLEMANN   1
2.   Open Secrets: Derrida and Negative Theology
        DAVID E. KLEMM   8
3.   Think Naught
        MARK C. TAYLOR   25
4.   How to Say No in French: Derrida and Negation in
     Recent French Philosophy
        EDITH WYSCHOGROD   39
5.   Modalism Revisited: Persons and Symbols
        JANE MARY TRAU   56
6.   Tillich and the Kyoto School
        LANGDON GILKEY   72
7.   Negation in Mahayana Buddhism and in Tillich:
     A Buddhist View of "The Significance of the History
     of Religions for the Systematic Theologian"
        MASAO ABE   86
8.   Response and Queries
        ROBERT P. SCHARLEMANN   100
9.   Replies
        DAVID E. KLEMM, MARK C. TAYLOR,
        EDITH WYSCHOGROD, JANE MARY TRAU,
        MASAO ABE   120
     Contributors   149
     Index   151

NEGATION AND THEOLOGY

ROBERT P. SCHARLEMANN

1

INTRODUCTION

TWO ASPECTS of the theological tradition seem to be at odds with each other. One is the identification of God with being itself—*Deus est esse ipsum*—with the implication that God is the one who just is and could not not be. The other is the identification of God with what is other than being and nothing. The first identification seems to equate God with pure positivity, to the exclusion of every trace of negativity; the second associates God with a certain kind of negativity, a negativity that on the one side needs to be distinguished from the pure positivity of being (as might be suggested by *esse ipsum*) and on the other side must not be equated with the pure nothingness of the *nihil*. Taken together, the two identifications prescribe a rule for thinking when the intended object of thought is the one named "God," one who neither is nor is not anything or nothing. Paul Tillich's *Systematic Theology* incorporated the two sides of this tradition in the concept of God as being-itself, the eternal negation of nonbeing—a concept that both Langdon Gilkey and Masao Abe discuss in their essays here—and in the symbol of the inaccessible holiness of Deity that shows itself both as divine and as demonic.

In view of this tradition, the question of negation and theology, or of the relation between God and the "not," is in one sense as old as theology. But, like other old thoughts, it is also as new as every effort to rethink it. A particular impetus has been given to that effort in recent years by the criticism of the ontotheological tradition, or the metaphysical identification of God and being, that was made in one way by dialectical theology—Karl Barth in particular—and in another way by Heidegger's and Derrida's deconstruction of metaphysical thought. These criticisms also converge with aspects of the dialogue with Buddhism, in which questions are raised from a different direction about the concepts of God and nothingness. Neither of the two terms, *theology* and *negation*, has a single sense. But, against the background of recent discussion, their combination indicates the direction of inquiry represented in the essays gathered here. Four indications of the direction of inquiry can be provided in this introduction.

The first indication is a distinction between negation as the saying of "No" and negation as a kind of judgment, opposite to an affirmative judgment. To say No to a proposal or question ("Shall we do this?" "No.") and to form a negative judgment ("Elms are not stones.") both involve a negation, but they represent different kinds of activities. In the sense of denying, or saying No, negation involves taking a stance toward what is proposed; it is a rejection of what is presented for acceptance or rejection. In the sense of forming a negative judgment, negation involves removing a certain attribute from a subject (or a subject from an attribute). A negative judgment is the "saying away" (*apo-phasis*) of a predicate from a subject, a separation of a predicate concept from a subject concept. A saying of No is a rejection of what is being proposed. The two are not unrelated. But there is a difference in the activities involved. In the one case, the activity is that of rejecting something proposed; in the other case, it is that of disjoining what has been joined in a proposition. But the result of both activities is the same to the extent that the "no" and the "not" point toward something other than what is in the proposal or proposition; they both create an opening toward something else than what is presented. As Edith Wyschogrod shows, however, the matter is even more complicated when we consider the manifold ways of saying No.

A second indication of direction is provided by the tradition of mystical theology, of which Dionysius the (Pseudo-)Areopagite became the virtual *doctor ecclesiae* in both Western and Eastern Christendom. Whether his work *Symbolical Theology*, to which he refers in his other writing, ever existed or remained only a project does not matter for understanding what Dionysius meant by negative theology. For his notion of symbolical theology incorporates negation into theology in a definite manner, motivated by the idea that the biblical imagery is a symbolism so designed that the human mind, oriented as it naturally is to the physical senses, can begin with things sensibly perceptible and move from them to the formless and from the formless to the things that point to the divine, which of itself both is and is not any of those things.

Mystical theology in this sense traces a path of thought from the positivity of the sensible world to the negativity of the formless to the symbolization that incorporates as well as exceeds the categories of the positive and the negative. David Klemm explicates this Dionysian notion and combines it with an analysis of Derrida that results in a suggestion concerning the complementary relation of hermeneutics and deconstruction.

A third indication of direction is provided by the concept of double negation, which plays a special role because of the turn given it by Hegel. Its significance is explored, though not with reference to Hegel, both by Wyschogrod's chapter and by Jane Mary Trau's chapter on the trinitarian conception of Deity which, in its own way, gives expression to the being of God as involving both a being and a not being. Hegel's innovation, at least over against the negation involved in analogical predication (in which negation meant denying the limitations implied in a predicate term applied to God) had to do with two matters, only one of which was theological. The first was the Kantian conception of moral freedom; the other, negative theology. It was in part the content of practical reason that occasioned Hegel's reflection. Ethical autonomy means that each subject is the free, originating agent of its own actions. Freedom cannot be thought of as a thing that one possesses in order to use or not to use. It must be thought of, rather, as that which is actualized in free actions. To act freely is to act in such a way as to be the origin—the source and beginning point—or the agent of the activity present in the activity itself. Kant could thus say that we can know freedom is real in the practical act itself, not as something that can be inferred from the act as necessary for its intelligibility but as something realized and known in the act itself. Where does the problem lie in this conception? It lies in the fact that, on the one hand, we are saying that freedom is radically individual, known in the exercise of it in practical activity (acting in accord with the moral law), and, on the other hand, that there is a universal process, other than the cause-effect process of nature, which is formulated as an unconditional moral law concretely expressed in the actions of an acting subject. If freedom is, really, a universal structure parallel to that of nature, then the practical experience of freedom as located in the individually acting human subject seems to be illusory; but if freedom is not such a universal structure, how can there be laws formulating it? The connection of this problem with negation was made by Spinoza's dictum *omnis determinatio est negatio*—every case of a universal is a negation of it. For this dictum appears to mean that there can be only one substance and that in it individuals must lose their individuality to be free. With respect to nature ("objectivity"), we can say there is only one nature but many things in nature; with respect to freedom ("subjectivity"), we are to say that freedom is equally real and universal (unconditional) in each of its instances. What negating of negation is involved in such a conception? Not a negation of negation which is equivalent to an affirmation (a negation of the individuality that negated the universality), but a different kind of double negation, one which breaks through the given framework of positive and negative. A crude, and possibly misleading, illustration of the two kinds of double negation can be seen by comparing "The leaf is not nongreen" (which means that it is green) with "The leaf is not nonslow" (which means, not that the leaf is slow, but that the opposites of "slow" and "fast" are not categories applicable to leaves at all).

Double negation therefore involves, as Hegel put it, an *Entgegensetzung gegen die Entgegensetzung*—an opposition against the opposition. In theological assertions, such double negation appears when categories of freedom and nature (or subjectivity and objectivity) are applied to God. One of the consequences following from Kant's critiques and the post-Kantian discussion was the recognition that there is no way of settling the metaphysical dispute between realism and idealism (are our ideas the reflections of reality, or is reality the construction of our ideas?). There is no way of settling it for the very reason that the intelligibility of the debate itself depends equally upon an ideal and a real element. But, if the irreducibility to one of the two principles of ideal and real (or subject and object, or self and world, or I and universe, and so on) is granted, the distinction between negation and double negation becomes decisively important. If there is no third, to which freedom and nature can be reduced, then God, as being beyond both freedom and nature, cannot be conceived of as a third kind of reality, from which both freedom and nature can be derived, but must be conceived through a double negation. To deny that God is freedom does not amount to affirming that God is nature. Rather, it is a double negation intended to break through the framework of being either the one or the other. Nature and freedom can be said to be *in* God, but God is not freedom (rather than nature) nor nature (rather than freedom). To say that God is not freedom would, in one sense of double negation, mean that God is nature; and to say that God is not nature would, similarly, mean that God

is freedom. This double negation would, in each of these two varia-
tions, amount to an affirmation. But in the other sense of double
negation, to say that God is not nature is not equivalent to saying
that God is freedom; and saying God is not freedom is not equivalent to saying God is nature. We seem here to be in the proximity
again of questions that Abe's essay illuminates, for the concern
there is to form a conception of the ultimate negative other than
as the concept of nonbeing which is derivative from being.

Finally, there is a fourth indication of the direction of questions
in these essays. It is the indication given by the "differing" that
has become a hallmark of Derrida and Derridans. It can be employed as a technique or strategy of saying something other, that
is, of speaking of the otherness of the other without reducing the
other to the same. Mark C. Taylor's essay both exemplifies and
discusses this strategy. We can contrast such a "differing" with the
technique of conversation or dialogue. In a conversation the aim
of the partners is to bring the reality under discussion to light by
the back and forth of affirmation, negation, and alteration of what
is said. Only through the yes-and-no of the actual discussion do
the partners come to understand what the conversation is about
and how each of them is related to it. This is the case regardless
of the result, whether it is an agreement or a disagreement among
them. The yes-and-no of such a conversation is similar to the thesis
and antithesis of a dialectic; but it differs because there is at the
start nothing common from which the thetical and antithetical
elements can be explicated. Unlike dialectical explication, con-
versations can take new and unforeseen turns and can bring in
matters not already implicit in the beginning. Through a dialectical explication, one can trace a movement of thought from the
thesis that "A is a" to the antithesis that "A is not-a" to the synthesis that "A is a and not-a (or is finitely a)"; for that one can use A
both as the subject and the predicate of a proposition implies that
there is both an identity and a difference in the A about which one
is speaking—if it is true that "A is a" it must also be true that "A is
not-a," and for both of those opposites to be true, each must serve
to limit the meaning of the other. Nothing is required for explicat-
ing those three elements beyond what is already logically implicit
in the first proposition. A conversation is different. The common
understanding it reaches, or the disagreement it discloses, is not
implicit in the beginning but emerges only in the course of the
conversation as new elements are injected into it by the partners.
Derrida's technique of "differing" is not such conversation or dia-

logue. The aim is always to differ with and from what another has said; it is, as it were, methodically to refuse conversation as a way of bringing into view that the different is always different from anything that might be said. This is the only way of knowing the otherness of the other, or the difference of *différance* as nonidentical even with itself. It does admittedly contain a trap; for when it becomes an expectable and even predictable use of technique, it results in communicating always the same and loses the difference of the different. Nonetheless, Derrida's technique, as it seems to me, makes us aware of the fact that conversation is exposed to the same problem as dialectic when it comes to speaking of the different as different or, in theological terms, when it comes to speaking of God as *totaliter aliter*, not just other than anything that is identical with itself but other than even the otherness that is the opposite of identity. The ways in which this recognition might be incorporated into the theme of negation and theology are explored particularly in the essays by Klemm, Taylor, and Wyschogrod. Trau's is concerned with some problems of being and not being in Deity that are associated with the trinitarian formulation. Gilkey and Abe give us a double discussion of the concepts of being and nonbeing in Christian theology and in Buddhism. Taken together, the several essays and the discussion they elicit cover some of the most basic perennial and contemporary questions.

Attention might be called, however, to the way in which the discussion of Tillich and Buddhism, in the contributions of Gilkey and Abe, both epitomizes the set of questions raised by negation and theology and also suggests a further avenue of exploration. Abe makes a point of the fact that in Tillich's ontological structure, being is finally given a certain priority over nonbeing; nonbeing is both logically and really dependent upon being. Gilkey, for his part, confirms this point by his analysis of Tillich and the Kyoto School. Unexpectedly this result brings to light another aspect of the question. The priority that Tillich ascribes to being over nonbeing, along with his identification of God with being-itself (the negation of nonbeing), is one that appears in the context of ontology or ontological analysis. That is to say, *if* the meaning of "God" is raised within the context of the structure of being, then the unity of being and nonbeing appears in the meaning of God as being-itself. But apart from the ontological structure (which is already the structure *of being*), and prior to the opposition of being and nonbeing, is the other opposition between being and (sheer) nothing. This opposition is expressed not by the difference between being and nonbeing, or between the "is" and the "is not," but by the difference between being and not, or between the "is" and the "not." In the context of an ontological structure (defined by the opposition of being and nonbeing), the concept of God (the ultimate, the unconditional) is the concept of something that mediates being and nonbeing with a priority to being. The priority, in Tillich's case, is both logical and real—God incorporates the negative as the power always already overcome, and the holiness of God incorporates both the creativity of the divine and the destructiveness of the demonic in an order that gives priority to the divine over the demonic; the life of God is, accordingly, a process of continually putting the negative into the past to which it belongs, of destruction taken into creations of the new. But the concept changes when the context is not ontology, or the structure of being, but that of the opposition between being and nothing. Abe is right, as it seems to me, in his analysis of Tillich's ontological theology. But the result could well be different if the discussion were directed to the concepts indicated in other works of Tillich. In 1919, for example, he wrote of "the absolute Nothing and the absolute Something" which is "simultaneously the No and the Yes" upon all things, which is not an entity, not the substance or totality of entities, but, "to use a mystical formulation, the Beyond-being that is simultaneously the Nothing and the Something." And Tillich adds, to forestall a misunderstanding, that even the predicate "is" is misleading here.[1]

With this we reach a place, in other words, where the question of negation and theology is shifted to a context other than that of ontotheology defined by the identity of God and being. It is a context in which one can not only see a side of the theological tradition often lost from view but also put the discussion with Buddhism, and its notions of negativity, onto a somewhat different and, one might suggest, a more promising ground.

NOTE

1. "Über die Idee einer Theologie der Kultur," in Gustav Radbruch and Paul Tillich, *Religionsphilosophie der Kultur* (1919; Darmstadt: Wissenschaftliche Buchgesellschaft, 1988), p. 36.

DAVID E. KLEMM

2

OPEN SECRETS:

Derrida and Negative Theology

THE QUESTION I want to pose offers no easy answer: Is deconstruction a version of negative theology for our postmetaphysical time? Indeed, the question is prompted by the open secret that Derrida can be read as a kind of crypto-theologian, whose writings offer a sophisticated negative version of the ontological argument for the existence of God. In this paper I want to interpret and assess the open secret of Derrida's hidden practice of negative theology. I do this in four steps.

First, I lay out one context in which to understand the relationship between Derrida's deconstruction and negative theology, namely, that of Karl Barth's twentieth-century interpretation of Anselm's eleventh-century ontological argument taken as a recovery of the *via negativa*. In this context, the language-event occurring through the name of God is said to make manifest the being of God as that than which none greater can be conceived. Following the line of thought set by this context, I turn to Derrida's recent work on negative theology to pose my question whether deconstruction is a new version of negative theology. My effort to understand leads to two interpretations of deconstruction: a hermeneutical reading in step two and a rhetorical reading in step three.

Both of these readings fail to comprehend deconstruction as a form of negative theology: Derrida's discourse successfully wards off both interpretations, because it resists the will to understand and with it the linguistic act of making sense of something in the form of a judgment. Deconstruction calls for understanding but eludes it. In step four, I make a tentative and experimental proposal that the very way deconstruction evades understanding means that Derrida's discourse cannot be a form of negative theology, for unlike negative theology it cannot incorporate reflective understanding into its own language-event. The discourse of deconstruction cannot embrace that than which none greater can be conceived by virtue of this exclusion. However, the very way deconstruction elicits understanding gives a clue for reconstructing negative theology by uniting it dialectically with hermeneutics, such that the double event of the overturning of deconstruction by hermeneutics and the overturning of hermeneutics by deconstruction itself gives linguistic appearance to that than which none greater can be conceived. I begin then with the first step: the context.

I

You recall the story of Anselm's own efforts to discover one argument sufficient in itself to prove that "God truly exists, and that God is the supreme good, needing nothing outside God's own being, but needful for the being and well-being of all things."[1] According to Anselm's testimony, the search became an obsession, which forced itself on the abbot, alternately bringing him hope and despair. "Then," he writes in the *Proslogion*, "one day, when I was worn out by my vigorous resistance to the obsession, the solution I had ceased to hope for presented itself to me, in the very turmoil of my thoughts, so that I enthusiastically embraced the idea which, in my disquiet, I had spurned."

Anselm addresses his answer to God, from whom Anselm believed the answer came. Writing from within the received faith of his community, Anselm claims, "We believe that thou art a being than which none greater can be thought." By so articulating his belief, Anselm reasons that a being than which none greater can be thought exists at least in his understanding. "But clearly that than which a greater cannot be thought cannot exist in the understanding alone," Anselm continues. "For if it is actually in the understanding alone, it can be thought of as existing also in reality, and this is greater." So, by the rule of greatness, "without doubt, therefore, there exists, both in the understanding and in reality, something than which a greater cannot be thought." The simple statement of faith is granted the understanding that God truly is; indeed, God cannot even be thought of as not existing. So goes Anselm's version of the ontological proof.

Karl Barth was mindful of Kant's devastating critique of the argument as an illicit attempt to derive existence from a concept of God, when in fact the assertion that something exists is never established by an inference from a necessary concept but rather requires an independent act of ascertainment through sensible experience.[2] Yet Barth was also mindful of Hegel's claim that there is something unique about the idea of God in that it alone is the idea of that which cannot be merely idea but must also actualize itself in reality.[3] There is something about the ontological argument that withstands Kant's critique, and Karl Barth attempted the following reformulation to bring it out.

According to Barth, in *Fides quaerens intellectum* (1930), Anselm's definition of God is not a definition at all.[4] The argument does not claim to be a deduction of the existence of God from a definition. The formula "that than which none greater can be thought" is strictly a noetic rule, a rule of thinking when one is thinking of God. According to Barth, Anselm received a negative prohibition on his thinking to the effect that when he thinks about God, he is to think of nothing greater. Anselm's formula does not tell us what God is. Rather, the text provides a rule of thinking which, when enacted, can make present the content of the words of the formula.

Barth's point is that the very act of following the rule will itself show the real existence of the one it names outside the thinking. Of course, the rule shows God negatively, by distinguishing God from everything else, including nothing: God is no thing, but God is not nothing either.[5] What comes into view by following the rule of thinking given in God's name? Nothing we can name, not even in the identity of thought and reality: God comes to those words by fulfilling or actualizing the sheer openness of both mind to reality and reciprocally of reality to mind. According to Barth, the words Anselm discovered are themselves the place where God's being is manifest, *ein Offenbarsein Gottes*, a being manifest on the part of God, which is not a question of logical necessity but a possibility depending on the good will of the thinker and the grace of the self-manifesting God.

What has this to do with Derrida? Readers of Derrida recognize his extraordinary capacity to disrupt established patterns of thinking and writing by disclosing the undecidability of texts. Systematically differentiating signified from signifier, he reveals in a negative way the power of language to construct a sense of self and world by undercutting stable relations between linguistic signs on one side and both the structures of thought as well as the reality to which thought refers on the other side.

"There is nothing outside the text" means that any appeal to a structure of thought or to real existence outside language must itself always depend on language. It does not assert that there is no reality outside language, but that thought and reality must come to language. With this recognition, the dominant paradigm of representational thinking comes to an end, according to Derrida.[6]

If the power of language exposed by Derrida's writings is taken not merely as a disruptive move but as an instantiation of the openness of mind to reality through language, then it is possible to view Derrida's writings as making manifest something like what Barth found in the words of Anselm—that than which none greater can be conceived—not of course by means of logical argument but by means of an enacted play of signifiers that point to and make perceptible the infinitely elusive being of God. Viewed in this way, the question arises concerning Derrida's relation to the tradition of negative theology and those influenced by it, from Pseudo-Dionysius to Barth.[7]

Where does Derrida place himself with respect to the *via negativa* in theology? Over the years, Derrida has argued vigorously that deconstruction is not a form of negative theology. In the essay "Différance," from 1968, Derrida warned that his notion of *différance* is not theological, "not even in the order of the most negative of negative theologies."[8] Nearly twenty years later, in a talk given in Jerusalem in 1986, entitled "Comment ne pas parler: Denégations" (or, in English translation, "How to Avoid Speaking: Denials"), Derrida felt obliged to address the question again. "No," said Derrida in Jerusalem, "what I write is not 'negative theology.'"[9]

The question remains open, however, because Derrida also admitted in both essays that one can find in deconstruction traits similar to those of negative theology. In "Différance," Derrida wrote that "the detours, locutions, and syntax in which I will often have to take recourse will resemble those of negative theology, occasionally even to the point of being indistinguishable

from negative theology."[10] In "How to Avoid Speaking," Derrida referred to a "family resemblance" between them, based on a "more
or less tenable analogy."[11]

   In other words, Derrida's own statements about the relation between his discourse and the discourse he identifies as negative
theology combine a denial with an affirmation of resemblance.
By so articulating the relation of his discourse to that of negative
theology, Derrida reproduces at a reflexive level the very relation
between the discourse of negative theology and the being of God.
Derrida's discourse is to the discourse of negative theology what
the discourse of negative theology is to God. Does this discourse
establish a real relation to God or only a parody of negative theology? In the remainder of my paper, I shall attempt to understand
in what way deconstruction can and cannot be understood as a
type of negative theology in our time.[12] I undertake this as a kind
of thought-experiment that is independent of what I might think
about more traditional and pre-postmodern forms of theology.

                                      II

Derrida says that deconstruction is *not* negative theology, yet he
affirms a resemblance. In my first attempt to understand the relation between the two, I explore the ground of the resemblance, to
interpret the "is not" between deconstruction and negative theology to mean deconstruction "is like" a negative theology. I call
the first reading the hermeneutical reading, and I begin it by focusing on what is in common between negative theology and deconstruction.

   For Derrida, negative theology refers to a textual practice situated in history whose strategies are driven by the claim that "every
predicative language is inadequate to the essence, in truth to the
hyperessentiality (the being beyond being) of God; consequently,
only a negative (*"apophatic"*) attribution can claim to approach
God and to prepare us for a silent intuition of God."[13] In this linguistic practice we have the common core between deconstruction
and negative theology, for both deploy the "negative determina-
tions" of *apophatic* discourse in moving toward an unknowable
goal—be it *différance* or God—which is also origin and cause of
the movement. What happens in the negative movements of language is in both cases an open secret. How so?

Most readers associate the tropics of negativity with dark utterances concerning the unsayable. We recall the ancient theme of
secrecy in sacred texts. Because the texts of Derrida abound in
apophatic discourse, they appear to participate in the tradition of
secret disclosure in religion. According to this theme, given the
difference between the being of God and human understanding,
sacred texts openly figure the divine in the form of secrecy. God's
word can only be heard by humans through the secret word that
sets apart, separates, or distinguishes (*secernere*) how or as what
God is not God. In other words, theological discourse must both
veil divine wisdom (since it cannot be spoken in propositions) and
unveil divine wisdom (by figuring it enigmatically).

What is the open secret of negative theology? I raise this question relative to Pseudo-Dionysius, whom Derrida selects as an
exemplar. I shall then ask, Can deconstruction accept the open
secret of negative theology? To attempt an answer to both of these
questions, I extend what Gadamer calls the "good will" of hermeneutics, by which he means the will through which one "does not
seek . . . to prove that one is always right, but one seeks instead
as far as possible to strengthen the other's viewpoint so that what
the other person has to say becomes illuminating."[14]

For Pseudo-Dionysius, God, "as Cause of all and as transcending
all, . . . is rightly nameless yet has the names of everything that
is."[15] Pseudo-Dionysius follows a twofold path of descent, from
the one to the many by way of affirmation, and ascent, from the
many to the one by way of denial. He begins by meditating on the
universal and eternal truths, such as the One, the Good, the Beau-
tiful, and Being, and then applies them to God as names, ascribing
them to God eminently and in essential unity. In saying, "God
is the Good," the mind directs itself to the transcendent divine
light that illuminates the light of the mind; its image is "the great,
shining, ever-lighting sun."[16] From the height of these conceptual
names, he descends toward the creaturely life as illuminated by
divine light.

The positive path is not adequate on its own, however. Recognizing that God so exceeds thought and speech that even the infinite extension of positive predicates falsifies God's being, Pseudo-
Dionysius reascends in a second moment by way of negation,
from lower and humbler names to the higher conceptual ones.
The negative way supplements the positive way by making clear
that although nothing strictly speaking can be ascribed to God,
everything in some sense can be ascribed to God "for everything

is good."[17] By denying the names derived from attributes found in
creatures, and denying the qualities abstracted from God, the way
of negation strips away all the human mind can say about God.
In this way Dionysius raises himself from the many names to the
One above language.

From the standpoint of hermeneutics, the secret of negative theology lies in the act of naming God, which, for Pseudo-Dionysius,
is itself the name of the unnameable. Robert Scharlemann and
others have shown how certain words, such as *I* and *God* are "instantiators." When put into action as words, they bring into being
the realities they name. Furthermore, these words instantiate their
meanings so as to be beyond the division between essence and
existence. Consider the case of *I* as instantiator: here the act of
determining *what* "I" am and determining *that* "I" am happen at
once in the saying. So also with the name "God," which instantiates absolute otherness in the very act of saying or thinking the
name: if I name "God," the universal subjectivity that is not-I and
not-this manifests itself through a negative manifestation that is
not nothing.[18]

Applied to the context of the Dionysian descent and ascent, in
saying now that "God is goodness," then, "God is not goodness";
or, now, "God is a stone," then, "God is not a stone," something
happens in and through the use of the language. Everything rests
on the divine name, which has the capacity to show the divine
otherness it names. In making affirmations and denials of God, the
divine otherness manifests itself alternately in connection with
both the *being* and the *nonbeing* of the intelligible or sensible
entity. The unnameable otherness shows itself as first the *same*
as the being named and then as *different* from the being named.
Taken in alternation, the being of God shows itself as the *unity* of
sameness and difference in the sensible and intelligible spheres,
as well as being *beyond* that unity.

The open secret of negative theology, in other words, is that
meditation on the divine names leads to God, not by prescribing
an agenda for thought or perception, but by opening a way in language. The secret is open, because the path is there for anyone who
speaks and hears; but it remains a secret, because people typically
look past language, concentrating on thoughts or intuitions. Thus
only few have ears to hear the divine name, much less the voice
to speak it. But it is to the words that Pseudo-Dionysius appeals.

The words themselves open up the secret "place" where God

dwells, as Pseudo-Dionysius describes it, by showing the negativity or otherness of God on the predicative connections that make of anything—goodness or a stone—both what it is and what it is not. However, to gain access to this place is not yet to contemplate God, Pseudo-Dionysius cautions. It situates the meditator in a place that is no place, a threshold to the divine, where he or she may be called "into the truly mysterious darkness of unknowing."[19]

Hermeneutically considered, the place in question is the linguistic understanding of being *as* being, the sheer openness of being to thinking and thinking to being. This openness *is* goodness, for it makes possible our naming anything at all, as well as our being named or called by name. The hyperessential God of negative theology, named as beyond being and nonbeing, comes to language as event when attention to the openness recedes, not for lack of volition, but in response to the advent of a divine darkness.[20]

Does this open secret of the divine names transfer to Derrida? Is *"différance"* somehow a divine name? This question may be undecidable, because *différance* neither names a perfection found defectively in entities and assigned supereminently to God, nor does it name any mundane thing at all. Whereas the theological name both veils and unveils, the Derridian sign eternally differs itself from other signs and defers meaning. Derrida refuses the name; he deconstructs the primacy of the spoken word in favor of the written sign. He refers the eternal play of signifiers to a nonlinguistic arche-writing, trace, or *différance*. *Différance* is neither a word nor a concept; it is not a name: *"Différance* is the non-full, non-simple, structured and differentiating origin of differences," which itself makes possible the functioning of every sign.

According to Derrida, in traditional conceptuality, *différance* would designate the original causality, but as the self-differentiating, playing movement of differences, "the name 'origin' no longer suits it."[21] Derrida claims that *"différance* governs nothing, reigns over nothing, and nowhere exercises any authority. It is not announced by any capital letter. Not only is there no kingdom of *différance*, but *différance* instigates the subversion of every kingdom."[22] *Différance* for Derrida manifests nothing, not even nothing, nor the not nothing. It cannot instantiate the principle of the goodness of being as such, because the trace or *différance* is for Derrida a first principle that is different from any principle, including itself, the principle that is no principle. *Différance* is "that which not only could never be appropriated in the *as such* of its name or its appearing, but also that which threatens the authority of the *as such* in general."[23]

How could Derrida accept a similarity between his discourse and negative theology? According to Derrida, negative theology still belongs to the "predicative or judicative space of discourse, to its strictly propositional form." Deconstruction, by contrast, is written "completely otherwise." It "calls for another syntax, and exceeds even the order and the structure of predicative discourse."[24] Hence for Derrida, deconstruction is not negative theology.

From the standpoint of hermeneutics, however, things still might be understood differently. Does uncovering the hermeneutical secret of the divine names in Pseudo-Dionysius enable us to read deconstruction as a version of negative theology, and in that way to correct Derrida? To this end, the hermeneutical inquirer might claim that the word *"différance"* can indeed be read speculatively as a symbol of the spirit of God, a symbol instantiating the motion of thought spiriting through the play of signifers. However, the hermeneutical proposal that deconstruction is a sophisticated form of negative theology must fail when submitted to Derrida's text for validation. Why is this?

If we turn to the texts of Derrida, and ask "Are you a form of negative theology?" they must answer "Not in any way that you can make out." Deconstruction cannot make interpretive judgments about the meaning of a text or an action, including itself as text or action, if it is to be true to *différance*. Thus deconstruction cannot both be negative theology and talk about itself as negative theology without giving itself up as deconstruction. The resemblance to negative theology to which Derrida points can only be to the purely negative side of negative theology. But negative theology works by way of interplay between positive and negative ways. Derrida's relation to the positive is purely parasitical; he cannot incorporate it. Thus he cannot speak about deconstruction in the way a negative theologian can speak about negative theology. Such judgments cannot be made by deconstruction. In its inability to reflect nondeconstructively, deconstruction clashes with both the hermeneutical project and with the tradition of theology influenced by the *via negativa*. The breakdown of understanding occurs in the meeting of wills.

According to Derrida's own testimony, the supposed "good will" extended by the voice of the other in reflective hermeneutics

masks an effort to annex the other into one's own world picture through the interpretive judgment.[25] To be true to *différance*,
Derrida construes the good will otherwise as the "good will to
power."[26] Herein lies a double bind. To be theologically meaningful, Derrida's text relies on having its reader interpret the movement of *différance* as a divine name with the "good will" of hermeneutics. But the good will Derrida's text requires from the reader
it must also deny of the reader, because the hermeneutical will to
understand is for him a will to power in disguise. And, ironically,
the will to power Derrida's text ascribes to the reader it must also
accept for itself, to the extent that Derrida's discourse appeals to
and thus wills to understand its reader.

The problem for deconstruction taken as a form of negative theology is that deconstruction cannot be theologically meaningful
by its own lights; it requires the light of another, which it must
deny. Deconstruction cannot admit to being a form of negative
theology. In trying to understand deconstruction *as* a form of negative theology, hermeneutics comes to naught. Derrida's discourse
evades understanding in a way that the discourse of negative theology does not. Derrida's discourse contradicts itself in a way that
the discourse of negative theology does not.

III

Perhaps, then, we should take Derrida more seriously when he asserts that deconstruction is not negative theology. Here I begin a
rhetorical reading. It takes Derrida's claim, that the good will is a
will to power in disguise, as a clue to deciphering the open secret
of Derrida's deconstruction. This reading is a suspicious one; it
seeks to uncover in Derrida's own discourse a motivating will to
power. By taking a rhetorical approach to Derrida's discourse, a
second possibility opens for reading the "is not" separating negative theology and deconstruction. In this reading, to say "deconstruction is not negative theology" means "deconstruction poses
as a post-metaphysical substitute for negative theology, but in fact
promotes only itself at the expense of the other."[27]

In the rhetorical reading, I focus on Derrida's Jerusalem talk, in
which he fulfills an earlier promise to explain directly his relation to negative theology. How did he do this? The suspicious
answer is that Derrida spoke about negative theology rhetorically,

rather than philosophically. The talk reenacts in present-day Jerusalem elements of the ancient Greek practice of *encomium*, in
which "the individual laid his entire life bare in the public square
of the *agora* to receive the civic stamp of approval of the whole
community, without which his life as a citizen would have been
incomplete."[28] In keeping with this type of discourse, Derrida gave
account of himself in response to the specific demands of a public
occasion: in this case, Derrida's long-expected advent to the Holy
City, where the promise to discuss negative theology had to be
fulfilled.

Derrida offers us good reasons to read the essay as a performance
of the rhetorical will to power: according to Plato in the *Gorgias*,
rhetoric as the art of persuasion becomes sheer manipulation when
it cannot articulate the "for the sake of which" it aims to persuade.
Without an orientation to the good, rhetoric is mere sophistry.

To what is deconstruction oriented? The telos of deconstruction is *différance* or undecidability, an undecidability that applies
even to itself as telos and erases the notion of telos. Whereas negative theological discourse is situated within ecclesial and contem-
plative communities whose sacred scripture, profession of faith,
and ritual activities orient its discourse to God and hermeneutical
discourse is situated within communities of understanding oriented by the norms inherent in communicative practice toward
the human good, the suspicion arises that deconstruction removes
itself from communicative practice within human communities.
Deconstruction cannot appeal to God or to the human good for
its orientation. As a form of persuasive discourse, deconstruction
cannot articulate its "for the sake of which" except as the erasure
of any "for the sake of which." Deconstruction's motivating obli-
gation is to be different; its mode of being is to be on the move,
to be as the wandering sophist or stranger, whose discomfort with
the world extends even to the nomadic existence it leads.

Lacking a subject matter, Derrida's rhetoric may tantalize with
the suggestion of theological profundity, but in fact it articulates
nothing other than the desire to persuade an audience. Derrida's
discussion of the "place" from which to understand his relationship to the God of negative theology disguises his real concern
with the "place" his thought will occupy in future discussions.

Read as sophistic, Derrida's essay makes sense. Derrida relates
himself to the past tradition as its postmetaphysical master. Derrida poses "deconstructive questions" to the classic texts by Plato,
Pseudo-Dionysius, and Heidegger. The aim is to disclose how each

of these three paradigmatic sites of negative theology remains determined by metaphysical discourse while preserving in spite of itself the trace of *différance.*[29] Derrida thereby demonstrates how deconstruction can dismantle the past tradition, while refusing the desire to enter the realm of predicative discourse or to pray to a hyperessential God.

Part of the rhetorical strategy for Derrida in this essay is to put himself on trial. He splits his identity between accusers and accused within a legal cross-examination during a mock "trial" (19), which he himself has constructed. "How to Avoid Speaking" includes juridical discourse, and in it Derrida engages in a subtle parody of the apology or legal defense before the *deme* in ancient Greece. Derrida faces "indictments" brought against him by his "accusers": three counts of dabbling in "negative theology."[30] The charges recall Socrates' crimes of impiety and corrupting the youth and possibly even the charge of blasphemy brought against Jesus.

After playing the role of the accusers in eloquently arguing the case against himself, Derrida switches his voice to that of defendant: "No, what I write is not 'negative theology.' " His dazzling deconstructions of Plato, Pseudo-Dionysius, Meister Eckhart, and Heidegger, reduce the charges to absurdity by showing that no one can write negative theology, because not even the negative theologians can write negative theology. Having erased negative theology, Derrida rests his case on the fact that he has no choice but to keep silent on negative theology, "even if put to the rack" and forced to confess through torture.[31]

Through his dismantling and mastery of the past tradition and his present evasion of the charge of negative theology, Derrida remains true to *différance* by controlling the future judgment about the place he will hold in the postmetaphysical pantheon. So reads the rhetorical analysis, as it deciphers the will to power.

Has the rhetorical reading tamed deconstruction? Is Derrida's open secret simply that the discourse of deconstruction is a subtle sophistic will to power? I think not. The rhetorical reading turns out to be just as vulnerable as the first hermeneutical reading when put to Derrida's text for confirmation. The reason is that the rhetorical reading still preserves a modicum of the will to understand, and thus is merely a suspicious variation of the first hermeneutical reading. In meeting the will to power with a will to power, rather than a "good will," the reader still aims to bring his or her will into correspondence with the will of the other. Derrida can ward off the charge of sophistry by answering that it is one more attempt to appropriate the other as the same. Derrida can say that deconstruction is different from what either the trusting or suspicious form of hermeneutics claims it to be; it has not been and cannot be understood.

IV

Deconstruction successfully invades and evades understanding: it calls to be understood, but resists understanding. But ironically the loss we recognize for hermeneutics in its struggle with deconstruction may be a gain for theology. Does the clash between deconstruction and hermeneutics help bring about a new negative theology? Let me explore the possibility by showing how each points to the other over a gulf.

Within the hermeneutical process, *différance* systematically confronts us with the extreme case of what Gadamer calls "the impenetrability of the otherness of the other."[32] By encountering *différance*, understanding suffers a reversal and an overturning at its limit. Exposure to *différance* places the self and its meaningful world at risk and in question.[33] The deconstructive breach between signifiers and their signifieds disorients us and drives to its limit what Gadamer calls the "negativity of hermeneutical experience."[34]

But deconstruction on its side likewise suffers an overturning and reversal at the limit in its own claim to be meaningful. Without addressing someone with an intention to be understood, deconstruction is an inaudible cry in the night. When Derrida names the self-differentiating play of signifiers "*différance*," the name which is not a name, he encounters the inevitability of the sameness of the same. The presence of identity of meaning connecting signs, sense, and reference reorients the self within a questionable and unstable world.

As primary textual practices, deconstruction and hermeneutics are different. Deconstruction is figured by the disruptive play of signs. Hermeneutics is figured by the continuity of meaning in the word. But despite the alterity between them, each linguistic practice can be overturned by the other. The disruptive play of signs is always susceptible of becoming a stable structure of meaning. A familiar and reliable meaning is always susceptible of being undone by setting its signs adrift. Through the overturning, each is referred back to itself and forward to the other: The unity of the word can in time be disrupted by the undecidability of the signifier-signified connection. The arbitrariness of the sign can always find stability in the word through conversational life in solidarity with others.

Moreover, despite the alterity between them, each seems to mirror the other inversely: deconstruction makes the familiar strange without losing its familiarity. Hermeneutics makes the strange familiar without losing its strangeness.

For the sake of playing out the theological possibility in these forms of discourse, let me venture this experiment. Perhaps the overturning relation between hermeneutics and deconstruction gives us a clue for reconstructing the open secret of negative theology at the reflexive level in which the relation between the discourse of a reader and that of a theological text reflects the relation in theological texts themselves between the discourse of the text and the God named by the text. With reference to the alternation between hermeneutical and deconstructive practices in reading texts, we can name God, in the style of Pseudo-Dionysius, as "the overturning" that occurs between meaning understood and meaning deconstructed. God is God as the overturning.

To say that God is God as the overturning is to say that in reading texts inscribed explicitly or implicitly with the divine name, the reader can alternately be brought to a clearing of meaning and to the unraveling of that meaning through the separation of linguistic sign and understood sense. To read the texts of negative theology both enables a reader to understand the divine and to understand that the divine exceeds understanding. Insofar as the language itself manifests the God who both comes to language and escapes it, the act of reading theological texts is itself a kind of enactment of the ontological proof, which relies on both hermeneutics and deconstruction to display the God who is God as the double overturning of the drift of signifiers by stable meaning and of stable meaning by the drift of signifiers.

If we extend the analogy with Pseudo-Dionysius by focusing on his use of a positive and negative way, we could say that the hermeneutical practice would thus form a new affirmative way of ascent to the one by means of unifying understanding through the divine name, and deconstructive practice would form a new negative way of descent to the many by means of disseminating signs through *différance*.

According to this reconstructed account, deconstruction cannot replace negative theology. But as a textual practice in combination with hermeneutics, it allows a reflexive refiguring of negative theology. In such a scheme, "God" would name the explicit overturning at the limit of both the negative and the affirmative ways—a name calling forth and judging discursive practices. At the hermeneutical limit of understanding, the name "God" presents the source and goal of meaning; it evokes and enables the event of taking responsibility for language by making interpretive judgments about the meaning and worth of human life. At the deconstructive limit of deferral, the name "God" presents *différance;* it chastens and judges our best efforts to grasp the meaning of life. The unity of the two senses of "God" would manifest the movement of thinking that aspires to God but ever fails to reach God. This event in language may be that than which none greater can be conceived—the goodness of being as such in which we live, move, and have our being.

The name "God" can work in this way and connect with the name "overturning" because "God" is both a *sign* (with no signified), as is Derrida's *différance,* and a *word* or *name* (which manifests meaning), as in theological hermeneutics. But we must hold in mind, while deploying such a divine name, that God literally *is not* what is named as the overturning. If God is being God in the overturning, God is also *beyond* the overturning as the overturning of overturning.

NOTES

1. Anselm of Canterbury, *Proslogion,* in *A Scholastic Miscellany,* ed. Eugene R. Fairweather (New York: Macmillan, 1970), pp. 69–74.
2. Immanuel Kant, *Critique of Pure Reason,* A592 / B620-A603/ B631.
3. Hegel, "Ausführung des ontologischen Beweises in den Vorlesungen über Religionsphilosophie vom Jahre 1831," *Vorlesungen über die Philosophie der Religion II, Werke,* vol. 17 (Frankfurt: Suhrkamp), pp. 528–35.
4. Karl Barth, *Fides quaerens intellectum* (Munich: Chr. Kaiser, 1931).
5. Barth is clear about the fact that we can have no positive knowledge of the reality that shows itself through the performance of this rule of thinking, for the rule prohibits our thinking of any*thing* by systematically transcending any specifiable content of thought in the direction of greatness. The thinker enacting the rule begins by entertaining the thought of God in the mind as a rule and is led by the rule from what Barth calls the circle of mental understanding to the circle of real existence outside the mind and from there to the circle of the identity of mind and reality with its attendant thought of the necessary existence of God. At the end of the proof, what we have is not universal and

necessary knowledge that God exists as the greatest of beings but a demonstration of God's being resulting from the exercise of distinguishing God from anything that can be thought by always thinking greater.

6. "In order to conceive of this age, in order to 'speak' about it, we will have to have other names than those of sign or representation. New names will have to be used [for] . . . the indefinite drift of signs, as errance and change of scene, linking re-presentations one to another without beginning or end" (Jacques Derrida, *Speech and Phenomena*, trans. David B. Allison [Evanston, Ill.: Northwestern Univ. Press, 1973], p. 103).

7. This theological tradition includes such alleged "logocentrists" as Thomas Aquinas, whose "way of remotion" holds that because "the divine substance surpasses every form that our intellect reaches, . . . we are unable to apprehend it by knowing *what it is.* Yet we are able to have some knowledge of it by knowing *what it is not.*" By distinguishing God from all that is, by means of negative differences such as the assertions "God is not a body," "God is not an accident," and the like, we distinguish God from all that God is not. Thus, says Thomas, "there will be a proper consideration of God's substance when God is known as distinct from all things" (*Summa contra Gentiles*, vol. 1: *God*, bk. 14, trans. Anton C. Pegis [Notre Dame: Univ. of Notre Dame Press, 1955]).

   Thomas is not content with the negative way alone, of course. He adds the way of analogy, by which certain perfections found in a limited way in creatures, perfections such as goodness and wisdom, can be predicated of God. Such predications can be made of God, from which they originate as first cause, and yet we cannot ascribe them to God as properties of a substance, for the divine substance is beyond composition and unthinkable by means of essential or accidental predication. To be God is to be unthinkable except by analogy, for to be God is simply to be. To assert that God is highest goodness or wisdom is to assert precisely that only God is God, while recognizing that we can only grasp what God is *not* while thinking that perfections found in creatures must be found in some supereminent and unthinkable way in God. Affirmations must be combined with denials when speaking about God (ibid., bks. 30–36).

8. Jacques Derrida, "Différance," in *Margins of Philosophy*, trans. Alan Bass (Chicago: Univ. of Chicago Press, 1982), p. 6.

9. Jacques Derrida, *Psyché: Inventions de l'autre* (Paris: Galilée, 1987), pp. 535–95. The English translation is by Ken Frieden: "How to Avoid Speaking: Denials," in *Languages of the Unsayable: The Play of Negativity in Literature and Literary Theory*, ed. Sanford Budick and Wolfgang Iser (New York: Columbia Univ. Press, 1989), pp. 3–70. The quotation is from p. 7.

10. Derrida, "Différance," p. 6.

11. Derrida, "How to Avoid Speaking," p. 4.

12. See Martin Heidegger, *Sein und Zeit*, pp. 148–49; *Being and Time*, tr. John Macquarrie and Edward Robinson (New York: Harper & Row, 1962), p. 189. In the tradition of Heideggerian hermeneutics, to work out that in terms of which something is figured as something is to work out the possibilities projected in understanding within the concrete situation at hand. Heidegger says the "as"-structure of understanding shapes the way we connect in language what we encounter with what we think of it. Because understanding is situated relative to a totality of involvements, is temporal and historical, and is tied to our being in the world, understanding generates new possibilities and remains irreducibly pluralistic. The linguisticality of understanding means both that being that can be understood is language and that we have no metaphysical standpoint outside of language from which to inspect what comes into being through language.

13. Derrida, "How to Avoid Speaking," pp. 3–4.

14. Hans-Georg Gadamer, "Text and Interpretation," in *Dialogue and Decon-*

struction: The Gadamer-Derrida Encounter, ed. Diane P. Michelfelder and Richard E. Palmer (Buffalo: State Univ. Press of New York, 1989), p. 55.

15. Pseudo-Dionysius, *The Divine Names,* in *The Complete Works,* trans. Colm Luidheid (New York: Paulist Press, 1987), p. 56.
16. Ibid., p. 74.
17. Pseudo-Dionysius, *Celestial Hierarchy,* in *Complete Works,* p. 150.
18. Robert P. Scharlemann, "The Being of God When God Is Not Being God," and especially "God as Not-Other: Nicholas of Cusa's *De li non aliud."* The first essay can be found in *Inscriptions and Reflections* (Charlottesville: Univ. Press of Virginia, 1989), pp. 30–53; the second is in *Naming God,* ed. Robert P. Scharlemann (New York: Paragon House, 1985), pp. 116–32.
19. Pseudo-Dionysius, *The Mystical Theology,* in *Complete Works,* p. 137.
20. Ibid., p. 141.
21. Derrida, "Différance," p. 11.
22. Ibid., p. 22.
23. Ibid., pp. 25–26.
24. Ibid., p. 4.
25. See Josef Simon, "Good Will to Understand and the Will to Power: Remarks on an Improbable Debate," in *Dialogue and Deconstruction,* p. 165.
26. Jacques Derrida, "Guter Wille zur Macht," in *Text und Interpretation,* ed. Philippe Forget (Munich: William Fink, 1984), pp. 56–58.
27. Derrida implies that deconstruction supersedes ontotheology: "*Différance* is not only irreducible to any ontological or theological—ontotheological—reappropriation, but as the very opening of the space in which ontotheology—philosophy—produces its system and its history, it includes ontotheology, inscribing it and exceeding it without return" ("Différance," p. 6).
28. Quotation from Rodolphe Gasché, *The Tain of the Mirror: Derrida and the Philosophy of Reflection* (Cambridge: Harvard Univ. Press, 1986), p. 143. The quotation follows closely M. M. Bakhtin, *The Dialogic Imagination,* trans. Caryl Emerson and Michael Holmquist (Austin: Univ. of Texas Press, 1981), pp. 130–35.
29. The trace is the already presupposed event, the very possibility of an experience of finitude, for which the distinction between finite and infinite is secondary. It is *différance,* and "the infinite *différance* is finite" ("How to Avoid Speaking," p. 29). See also Derrida, *Speech and Phenomena,* p. 102.
30. Speaking in the voice of nameless accuser, Derrida says to himself, first, "You prefer to negate; you affirm nothing; you are fundamentally a nihilist." Second, "You speak only for the sake of speaking, in order to experience speech." Third, "Your constant negating, in saying X is neither this nor that, constitutes a discourse in which every sentence would be already haunted by the name of God" ("How to Avoid Speaking," pp. 5–6). Another set of indictments is found on p. 19, reminiscent of Socrates' distinction between his "earliest" and "most recent" accusers in the *Apology.*
31. "How to Avoid Speaking," p. 16.
32. Gadamer, "Text and Interpretation," p. 27.
33. In this regard, deconstruction shows us what is always happening in the experience with language, when we encounter the *Sache* which leaves speechless and vulnerable. See Gerald L. Bruns, "On the Tragedy of Hermeneutical Experience," *Research in Phenomenology* 18 (1988): 191–201.
34. By this phrase Gadamer conceives of genuine experience as the painful recognition of our human finitude and the depths of our self-estrangement. At the same time, the experience of the negativity for Gadamer is also energizing, liberating, and enlightening. "Openness for new experience" is the measure of any experience (Gadamer, *Truth and Method,* 4th ed. [New York: Continuum Books, 1974], pp. 318–20).

3

THINK NAUGHT

... anti-anti-art, non-non-art, non-expressionist, non-imagist, non-surrealist, non-primitivist, non-fauvist, non-futurist, non-figurative, non-objective, non-subjective, non-action, non-romantic, non-visionary, non-imaginative, non-mythical, non-organic, non-vitalist, non-violent, non-vulgar, non-naturalist, non-supernaturalist, anti-accident, anti-brute-junk-pop-folk-art, non-local, non-regionalist, non-nationalist, non-representational ...

AD REINHARDT

THE QUESTION that remains after (the) all has been said is how to think naught otherwise than by not thinking. Nothing is, after all, always the question. The interminable question of the after-all is not original but repeats in a different register the question of the before-all. This repetition does not produce a mirror image in which beginning and end complete the circuit of reflection that encloses and ensures the completion of thought. To the contrary, nothing interrupts reflection. The naught that breaks the circuit of reflection cannot, however, be thought as such. Thought, therefore, remains forever incomplete. To think naught otherwise than by not thinking it is necessary to think that which "is" neither being nor nonbeing.

How to begin? Where to begin an unthinking that is not simply thoughtless? Perhaps with vision. If, as the history of Western philosophy and theology suggest, thought and vision are inextricably bound together, then to think naught might be to envision nothing.

Visualize naught. What color are you seeing or thinking? What color is nothing? Nothing is, of course, colorless. What color, then, is colorlessness or the absence of color? Though the question is impossible, it does (impossibly) have an answer: the color of colorlessness or the absence of color is black. Visualize black . . . Imagine nothing . . . nothing but black. Nothing seems easier . . . nothing more simple. But is black really so simple? Can black be represented or is it nonrepresentational?

Dark

"Black", medium of the mind . . .

Leave temple images behind
Risen above beauty, beyond virtues, inscrutable, indescribable
Self-transcendence   revealed yet unrevealed

Undifferentiated unity, oneness, no divisions, no multiplicity
No consciousness of consciousness

All distinctions disappear in darkness
The darkness is brilliance   numinous, resonance[1]

These words were written by Ad Reinhardt, a leader in the post–World War II movement of art known as Abstract Expressionism and a lifelong friend of Thomas Merton. Reinhardt, like his fellow painters Mark Rothko and Barnett Newman, was obsessed by the spiritual dimensions of nothing or nonbeing. Reinhardt's artistic career culminated in a thirteen-year struggle to represent the unrepresentable by painting nothing. For Reinhardt, to paint nothing was not not to paint. Though he shared the preoccupation with an end of art common among twentieth-century artists, Reinhardt resisted Duchamp's dramatic gesture of overtly (though not covertly) ceasing to produce works of art. From Reinhardt's point of view, the end, that is, both the cessation and the goal, of art is the overcoming of representation.

To understand the importance of Reinhardt's position, it is necessary to realize that from its beginnings in ancient Greece, Western art has been representational. While the interpretation of representation has changed repeatedly over the years, its structure has remained remarkably consistent. Within the economy of representation, a signifier is supposed to render transparently present a signified from which it emerges and to which it refers. In terms of the work of art, the image re-presents the thing or idea for which it stands. The better the image, the fuller is the presence of the signified in the signifier. Though usually overlooked or repressed, there is an inherent contradiction in the structure of representation. What is intended to be the re-presentation of the signified in the signifier is actually the de-presentation of the thing or idea in the image. Instead of the realization of presence, the image is the inscription of absence.

The recognition of the failure of representation is one of the primary insights of modernism. In a variety of ways, modern artists attempt to negate absence and realize presence by overcoming the contradictions involved in representation. In the visual arts, one of the forms of the quest for essential presence is nonobjective or abstract painting. There are, of course, many versions of abstract art: Picasso's cubism, Kandinsky's nonobjectivism, Malevich's suprematism, Mondrian's neoplasticism, LeWitt's conceptual art, Morris's minimalism, etc. What unites these otherwise diverse artistic tendencies is their shared suspicion of representation. No longer an ideal to be pursued, representation becomes a problem to be resolved. The structure of representation renders impossible the enjoyment of total presence for which the artist longs.

Nowhere is the critique of representation more radically embodied than in Reinhardt's Black Paintings. From 1954 to 1967, Reinhardt attempted to carry the process of abstraction to its most extreme conclusion by painting a series of seemingly identical black canvases. These paintings are, in my judgment, the most powerful statement of negative theology that has been developed in the twentieth century. In these paintings, one can see both the rich potential and the inescapable difficulties of the *via negativa*.

To claim that Reinhardt's final project is an exercise in negative theology is not to impose alien theological categories on an artistic undertaking. Throughout the latter part of his career, Reinhardt insisted that his artistic purpose was "to retrieve the spiritual in a secular culture."[2] The goal of this enterprise is what Eckhart describes as "the divine dark." Reinhardt's movement toward this sacred darkness is a "mystical ascent" to nothing.

Mystical ascent { *- separation from error, evil*
- " from world of appearances, sense attractions
-"The divine dark"—"luminous darkness"[3]

The telos of the mystical quest is perfect oneness with "the divine dark." The method Reinhardt uses in his ascent is the process of negation. Reformulating Mies van der Rohe's well-known modernist dictum, "Less is more," Reinhardt maintains that "Less in art is not less. More in art is not more." To approach the less that is not less but more, it is necessary to effect a separation from the world of appearances. This separation is realized through the activity of abstraction. For Reinhardt, negation *is* abstraction. Abstraction removes every vestige of form and figuration in order to reach the formlessness of the unfigurable or unrepresentable. The erasure of form and figure is supposed to leave the trace of an original oneness. This oneness is lost with the emergence of form and the inscription of figure. While the presence of form is the absence of oneness, the absence of form is the presence of oneness. Form necessarily entails difference and difference negates oneness. To approach the One that is the arche and telos of the cosmic as well as the artistic process, it is necessary to negate negation by means of abstraction.

Reinhardt's use of abstraction as a method of negation repeats one of the most important strategies employed by early Greek philosophers in their search for the original One from which all emerges and to which everything longs to return. Developing insights advanced in Plato's *Parmenides*, Speusippus proposes a novel way of negation that he labels *aphairesis*, or abstraction. Aphairesis is intended to be an alternative to the well-established method of *apophasis*.[4] As the identification of the *via negativa* with apophatic theology suggests, apophasis is usually the form of negation used in traditional negative theology. Apophasis negates by stating an opposite. X, for example, is identified as not-Y. Such negation, however, remains somewhat indefinite, for it determines X only in relation to a specific entity or quality. Complete identification would require an infinite series of negations. Aphairesis, by contrast, negates by abstracting or subtracting particular qualities from an entity. The penultimate aim of aphairesis is the essence of the entity under consideration; its ultimate aim is the essential One that underlies the many that comprise the phenomenal world.

In its early versions, aphairetic negation presupposes an interpretation of the creation of the cosmos through a prolonged process in which layers of reality gradually accumulate. From the time of the Pythagoreans, this creative process was interpreted in terms of mathematics and geometry. The primal One generates numbers, which, in turn, give rise to points, lines, planes, and eventually solids. These geometrical forms constitute the structural foundation of everything.[5] Each additional layer is, in Pythagorean terms, a supplementary "prosthesis." As the ground of grounds, the One is the absolute origin from which later prostheses derive. Aphairesis reverses this creative process by removing or stripping away successive supplements. By progressing from the world of appearances to the realm of forms and then proceeding from solid to plane to line to point, it is possible to approach the One. Since supplements corrupt the origin, they must be erased or at least seen through if the True or the Real is to be discovered. Aphairesis functions like a "ritual purification" that allows the initiate to draw near the purity of the origin. This origin is the "darkness" that mystics deem divine.[6]

With this darkness, we return to Reinhardt's Black Paintings. Black, I have suggested, is the color of colorlessness—the color of the absence of color. In Reinhardt's words:

"Black", absence *of* "color", colorlessness, *darkness*, lightlessness
Art of "painting" *vs. art of color (color-engineer, psychologist)*
"Painting is black, sculp. is white, arch. is color"

Black as color, *shiny black on matt black, texture, scumble,*
   "Color blinds"   *contrast*
   "Color sticks in one's eyes like something caught in one's throat"
   "Colors are an aspect of appearance and so only of the surface"
   "Manifest an indiscreet personality with shameful insistence"
   Colors are barbaric, unstable, primitive, "woven into the
      fabric of life," cannot be completely controlled, "and
      should be concealed"
"Blacked-out", non-color,   *beyond color, shape, line*
Monochrome, monotone, *Chinese, Guernica*

Negative *presence,* "darkness", *"a getting rid of"*, "blowing out"
Diminishing, beyond shapes, colors, "melting away,"
Dematerialization, *non-being*[7]

The absence of color is not, however, mere absence but is at the same time a hidden presence. The absence of color embodied in black is actually the result of the absence or total absorption of light. Black, in other words, issues from the *total presence* of light. The darkness of this light and light of this darkness offer illumination for those with eyes to see.

While black is the total presence of light that results from complete absorption, white is the absence of light that is a function of perfect reflection. That which reflects or transmits light perfectly lacks light and thus in itself is dark. If black is the total presence of light and white the complete lack of light, then dark appears light and light appears dark. The coincidence of light and dark is implied in the obscure etymology of the word *black*. "Old English, *blæe, blac;* Old High German, *blah-, blach-* (in combination); a word of difficult history. In Old English, found also . . . with long vowel *blace, blacan,* and thus confused with *blac* shining white: Old Teutonic *blaiko* . . . as is shown by the fact that the latter also occurs with short vowel, *blac, blacum;* in Middle English, the two words are often distinguishable only by the context and sometimes not by that."[8] When black is white and white is black, we glimpse a "point of indifference" in which differences collapse into primal unity.

This point of indifference is the return of the Parmenidean One for which mystics and negative theologians ceaselessly search. As the ground of being, this original One does not exist *sensu strictissimo.* Nor is it simply nonbeing. The One is "beyond being."[9] Forever beyond, the One resists positive predication and hence eludes kataphatic theology. The only way in which the One can be affirmed is through negation.

It would be a mistake, however, to think that the One beyond being breaks with or disrupts the economy of ontotheology. While sometimes defined in terms of nothingness or nonbeing, the One is actually "hyperreal" or "surreal." Though beyond being, this surreality lends being to whatever exists. Inasmuch as the surreal One is the primal origin of everything, it remains implicated in the order of being. This ongoing implication calls into question the difference between kataphatic theology on the one hand, and, on the other, apophatic and aphairetic theology. Though apophasis and aphairesis reverse or invert the structure of kataphatic theology, they do not subvert the essential presuppositions of Western philosophy and theology. To the contrary, the quest for the surreal perpetuates the ontotheological tradition that extends from Parmenides, Plato, and Plotinus to Reinhardt and beyond to many philosophers, theologians, and artists in our own day.

Reinhardt shares with his Neoplatonic precursors the desire to be united with the Origin. If this union is to be consummated, the forms and figures that are the prosthetic supplements separating one from the origin must be removed. When abstraction is com-

plete, union is achieved in the total darkness of the black canvas.
In a revealing poem entitled simply "One," Reinhardt writes:

> *"Formless thou art, and yet*
> *thou bringest forth many forms, and then*
> *withdrawest them to thyself."*

> *"Differentiating itself and yet remaining in itself*
> > *undifferentiated."*

> *"By letting go, it all gets done =*
> *the world is won by those who let it go!*
> *But when you try and try*
> *the world is then beyond winning."*

> *"in the beginning is the end," vice versa ←*

> *Ultimate diagram, free space, universal dimension*
> *Last word, to the end*   *"mania for totality"*
> *Triumph over time, death, oblivion "a fragrance of eternity"*
> *Totality, unity, finality*   *wordless essence*[10]

Mania for totality . . . unity, finality . . . wordless . . . imageless
essence. Does the end, which is the beginning, ever arrive? Reinhardt did not paint *one* black canvas but many. He intended each
work in this series to be "the last painting one can paint." And yet
there were more . . . always more. The last painting would be the
end of abstraction. This end must be understood in at least two
ways. In the first place, Reinhardt's Black Paintings would complete the movement of abstraction that has dominated twentieth-
century painting. While Picasso leaves planar forms, Kandinsky
and Mondrian geometric structures, Rothko misty hues, and Newman "zipped" color fields, Reinhardt aspires to pure formlessness.
The unrepresentable, he believes, can be represented only by the
absence of form and figure. The *absence* of form is the *presence* of
divine formlessness. This formlessness points to the second way
of understanding the end of abstraction. The telos of abstraction is
the unveiling of the total presence of the One from which the many
devolve. This end *is* truly the beginning. To paint the last painting
is to complete the archeoteleological process that constitutes the
history of the West.

But Reinhardt fails. Instead of realizing the end of abstraction,

his Black Paintings imply the impossibility of union and the in-
accessibility of the One. Abstraction, it seems, is endless. Reinhardt's inability to overcome representation is evident in the repetition of his dark canvases. Never satisfied with his depiction of the
plenitude of the void, Reinhardt is compelled to reiterate his aphairetic painterly gesture. This repetition or reiteration reinscribes
the absence of the very presence it is intended to realize.

This irrepressible absence emerges not only between seemingly
identical paintings but can also be discerned on the painted surface
of individual works. At first glance, Reinhardt's Black Paintings
appear to be monochromatic. The process of abstraction seems to
result in a uniform black surface from which all differentiation
has disappeared. Closer inspection, however, reveals differences
that are all too easily overlooked. Reinhardt's canvases are not
precisely monochromatic. Rather, each surface is created by the
subtle interplay of different hues. Shades of deep reds, browns,
blues, and lavenders mingle to produce the darkness that fills the
painted surface. When mixed on Reinhardt's palette, black is not
merely the negation or absorption of colors. His Black Paintings are
not simple but are richly complex. Moreover, as one contemplates
the shades of difference on the canvas, shifting patterns begin to
emerge and withdraw. Just as the Black Paintings are not really colorless, so too they are not utterly formless. In the shadows of the
dark canvases, subtle geometric patterns can be dimly discerned.
Since the retreat into formlessness is incomplete, differences abide
and oneness withdraws.

Though not immediately apparent, the unexpected complexity
of Reinhardt's late paintings implies a critique of the philosophical and theological presuppositions that inform his art. By tracing
the outlines of this critique, it is possible to identify a theological
alternative that is neither positive nor negative.

We have discovered that Reinhardt's strategy of negation repeats
the aphairetic activity of abstraction through which one tries to
return to the primal origin by reversing the process of supple-
mentarity. The accretion of prosthetic supplements carries one
farther and farther from the creative origin. The relation between
origin and supplements is completely ambivalent. While the surreal origin bestows being on everything that exists, the play of
supplements introduces differences and duplicity that threaten to
corrupt the pure oneness of the hyperreal.

In the wake of the failure of Reinhardt's painterly project, it
is necessary to rethink the relation between origin and supple-

Ad Reinhardt, *Abstract Painting*, 1963.
(Collection of Williams College Museum of Art)

ment, as well as oneness and difference. Reinhardt's written texts and spoken pronouncements make it clear that he stands firmly within the Western ontotheological tradition according to which oneness is ontologically antecedent to, and the condition of, the possibility of difference. This ontological priority is reflected in a hierarchy of values in which unity is privileged over plurality. In contrast to his verbal expressions, Reinhardt's paintings invert and, more importantly, subvert classical ontology and axiology. Rather than oneness creating difference, the play of differences on the surface of the canvas generates the appearance of a unified field in which oneness seems to absorb multiplicity. The origin, then, is not original but is a supplement to supplements. In the shadows of Reinhardt's obscure paintings, nothing remains but the differential play of supplements. This play simultaneously calls forth and frustrates the mania for totality . . . unity . . . finality . . .

·   ·   ·   ·

A haunting trace remains. In several of the Black Paintings, a startling form emerges from the shades of darkness—it is the figure of the cross. Perfectly symmetrical, the cross divides the canvas. There is something mysterious—even uncanny—about this cross. Not only is it obscure and elusive; more puzzling, it does not seem to have been painted. The cross bears no trace of its origin; the brush strokes have left no marks. How is this remarkable figure to be read? Does it harbor a vision of the sacred that has until recently remained unthought?

·   ·   ·   ·

Throughout its history theology has, of course, taken many forms. And yet the alternatives have always been simple: positive or negative. Since the Enlightenment, confidence in humankind's ability to make positive assertions about God or the absolute has waxed and waned. While some believe that the autonomy of reason makes it possible to unravel every mystery—divine as well as human—others are convinced that the free exercise of reason encounters limits that cannot be surpassed. In the twentieth century, self-confident reason and self-doubting skepticism form a strange alliance in relation to theological matters. The will to truth that religion has long nourished turns against religion itself. The very reason that once sought to comprehend divine mysteries now assuredly proclaims that religion is an illusion and God is nothing. From this point of view, the overcoming of religion and the death of God leave people free to realize previously unimagined possibilities. It is obvious that this situation can be interpreted differently.

In the absence of the divine or absolute, the cosmos, it might be argued, becomes unintelligible. Instead of a fetter to human reason, God who is, after all the Logos, can be understood as the guarantor of the power of reason and the rational order of the universe. From this point of view, the death of God marks the disappearance of reason. Humankind is left to err aimlessly in a dark void.

Theologians have responded to the penetrating criticisms of rationalists and skeptics in a variety of ways. Conservatives react by trying to reassert established dogmas and pieties. Liberals struggle to formulate an effective compromise by accommodating traditional beliefs and practices to the present situation. Radicals embrace the death of God as the culmination of the incarnational process.

There is, however, another response to the modern critique of religion that theologians have been slow to appreciate. While influential rationalists and skeptics claim that God is nothing, some of this century's most important artists believe that nothing is divine. Through a dialectical reversal, the absence of God becomes the presence of the divine. This presence is a negative presence—though a presence nonetheless. As theologians gradually recognize the significance of the artistic refiguration of the religious, there is growing interest in negative theology. If the *via positiva* is a dead end, then a restructured *via negativa* might open an alternative route to God. Perhaps. But is the negative really an alternative to the positive, or are the positive and the negative two versions of the same alternative? Somewhere Kierkegaard avers: "To do the opposite is also a form of imitation." Reinhardt's Black Paintings seem to support Kierkegaard's claim. Though his paintings are implicitly critical of the fundamental assumptions of classical theology and not obviously religious, Reinhardt, as we have seen, remains within the ontotheological tradition. The divine is the original presence that is the abiding ground and eternal telos of the cosmic process. As the primal source of all forms, the divine itself is formless. Determinate images and shapes negate original plenitude by introducing difference into indeterminate oneness. To recover the origin, negation must be negated by erasing every form and figure. With the negation of negation, the negative is transformed into the positive. In this way, the *via negativa* reverses itself to become the *via positiva*. Within this framework, the negative is not thought radically but is interpreted as a transitory moment that prepares the way for a higher positivity. Absence becomes presence, emptiness becomes fullness, death becomes life. In spite of these transi-

tions, nothing really changes. With the recognition of the identity
of the *via negativa* and the *via positiva,* theology reaches its end.

If nothing really changes . . . if theology has exhausted its possibilities, the question that remains to be asked is posed by Beckett:
"Is there really nothing new to try? I mentioned my hope, but it
is not serious. If I could speak and yet say nothing, really nothing? . . . But it seems impossible to speak and yet say nothing, you
think you have succeeded, but you always overlook something."[11]
Is there really nothing new to be tried? Perhaps the new to be
tried "is" nothing. Perhaps nothing can be tried anew. Perhaps it is
still necessary—or possible for the first time—to ask how to think
naught otherwise than by not thinking. Theology has, in a certain
sense, reached its closure. Though it continues, theology is as dead
as the God for which theologians search. Efforts to the contrary
notwithstanding, the *via negativa* cannot resurrect divine presence in the midst of overwhelming absence. The failure of the *via
negativa* is, in large measure, the result of the ongoing resistance
to thinking naught. The nothing or nonbeing of negative theology
is, in the final analysis, identical with being. To think naught radically, it is necessary to think that which is *neither* being *nor* nonbeing. Within the closed economy of ontotheology, the naught that
eludes the alternative of being or nonbeing is even less imaginable
than the nothing that is the opposite of everything.

It has often been observed that words—even Reinhardt's own
words—cannot do justice to his Black Paintings. The converse has
not been noted: Reinhardt's paintings betray his words. He paints
the impossibility of the formlessness and oneness that his words so
eloquently describe. This impossibility figures the impossibility
of theology as such. To think the naught that is neither being nor
nonbeing is to think the impossibility of theology. This impossibility is marked and remarked in the play of differences that cross
and crisscross the darkness that surrounds and invades us.

The site, which is really a nonsite, of the dark cross is sacred.
But what *is* the sacred? It is impossible to answer this question, for
its "is" presupposes precisely the ontology that the neither / nor
of the sacred renders problematic. The sacred does not exist; nor is
it simply nonexistent. Unlike the divine or absolute, the sacred is
not being itself or the ground / origin of being; nor is it nonbeing
or nothing. More negative than the negative that is the opposite
of the positive, the sacred haunts the boundaries, margins, and
interstices of structure, form, and figure. Never present without
being absent, the sacred haunts the structures it forever eludes.

The relentless proximity of the sacred interrupts every beginning and puts an end to all ending.

To think the naught of the sacred is not not to think but is to think endlessly. Such endless thought does not erase form and figure in order to overcome the regime of representation. There is no exit from the order of representation, yet that order is incomplete—necessarily incomplete. To think this incompletion is to ·think the naught that is "inside" as the "outside" that forever dislocates everything that would be itself. Such thinking figures the unfigurable by thinking and rethinking the failure or fault of structure—be that structure psychological, social, cultural, political, artistic, or religious. Along this fault the approach of the sacred can be discerned. Structures are constructed and gods are created to mend this fault and thus repress the sacred. But the repressed returns—returns eternally.

Since the sacred escapes the strictures of ontotheology, it can be reached by neither the *via positiva* nor the *via negativa*. It can be thought, if at all, in a non-negative negative a/theology that is nonetheless not positive. Unthinkable thoughts that approach along the margin that both joins and separates positivity and negativity call into question everything once deemed divine. In the wake of the eclipse of the divine, darkness . . . sacred darkness lingers . . . lingers endlessly.

> *Night*
> *Sacred night*
> *Night that is not day*
> *Night beyond*
> *Night*
> *Night*
> *From which we never*
> *Awake*

NOTES

1. Ad Reinhardt, *Art-as-Art: The Selected Writings of Ad Reinhardt*, ed. Barbara Rose (New York: Viking, 1975), p. 89.
2. Ibid., p. 82.
3. Ibid., p. 105.
4. In developing the following remarks, I have been guided by Raoul Mortley's

Word to Silence: The Rise and Fall of the Logos, vol. 1–2 (Bonn: Hanstein, 1986).

5. This insight suggests a relationship between aphairesis and the geometricism that informs movements in modern painting like cubism and neoplasticism as well as the dominant movement in modern architecture—International Style.
6. Mortley, *Word to Silence*, 2:42.
7. Reinhardt, *Art-as-Art*, p. 95.
8. *Oxford English Dictionary*.
9. Mortley, *Word to Silence*, 2:89.
10. Reinhardt, *Art-as-Art*, p. 92.
11. Samuel Beckett, *The Unnameable* (New York: Grove, 1958), p. 20.

4

HOW TO SAY NO

IN FRENCH:

Derrida and Negation

in Recent French Philosophy

THE ENGLISH language is rich in affirmation, poor in negation whereas, by contrast, French is replete with expressions of denial and limitation. In English, *no* and *not* are the primary particles expressing denial. "No, I shall stay right here," expresses a negative conatus, the refusal to undertake an action, whereas the *no* of "There are no cookies in this jar" is a numerical concept setting forth the absence of numerable objects. The *not* of "He is not an English gentleman" is part of a taxonomical or class term signifying those who are and are not English gentlemen whereas the *not* of "Thou shalt not covet thy neighbor's goods" is a proscriptive particle. Sometimes *no* and *not* are interchangeable as in "There are not any cookies" or "There are no cookies" in this jar, but a foreigner mistaking "He is not an English gentleman" for "He is no English gentleman" would have committed a serious social gaffe. Temporal negation indicated by the term *never* is simply a composite of the negative particle *not* with *ever* whose root, *aiw*, has two primary meanings: vital force and eternity.

By contrast, French expressions of negation are often composites. Thus, for example, the French *ne* combines with *pas* to mean not, "Je ne veut pas marcher," with *de* to mean always, "Il ne cesse de gronder," or with *que* to mean only, "Il n'a dit que cela," with *plus* to mean again, "Je ne le crains plus." The *not* of numeration or of nullity and void is expressed by *nul / nulle*, which also as a pronominal form means nobody. But what is one to make of the temporal locution *jamais*, a composite of *ja* as in *déjà*, already, and *mais* in the Latin sense of *magis*, or more? Is the *ja* of *jamais* always already inside the whole of time, inside it in a deconstructive sense, as leaving a trace of the never's having passed through its opposite, eternity, whose root is *aiw*, the same as the root of the English *ever*? Of special significance in the present context as Derrida explains is that the *ne pas* of "Comment ne pas dire?" can mean how not to speak in general or how to avoid an aberrant or incorrect meaning.[1] These sketchy etymological reflections are intended only to suggest linguistic differences that articulate anterior metaphysical orientations. As Derrida shows in *"Ousia* and *Gramme,"* it is not a question of arguing for the linguistic determination of metaphysical constructs but rather of showing how well-established metaphysical protocols are reflected in language, a language that can be pressed into a self-deconstructing speech, speech about the avoidance of speaking, what Derrida calls the "apophatics of denial."[2]

This difference, the difference between simple forms of negation and a nuanced and inflected conceptual negation is reflected in the structure of English and French philosophy, in the generally optimistic tone of Anglo-American social thought from Locke, Bentham, John Stuart Mill and G. E. Moore to William James, G. H. Mead, Dewey, and Rawls in contrast to the skeptical and cynical cast of French ruminations on the nature of society from La Rochefoucauld, Montaigne, Voltaire and Diderot to Sartre. Hobbes and Rousseau, among the most complex and original thinkers of their respective traditions, constitute notable exceptions to the tenor of these standard mind-sets. Perhaps the task each set himself was framed by the problematics of avoidance: how to avoid speaking the nation's metaphysical idiom by speaking in the metaphysical language of the other. It could be argued that Rousseau's trip to Derbyshire in 1766 and his confrontations there with Hume reflected a prior desire for the not, not to philosophize in French, metaphysically speaking, but in a polyglot in which the traces of an Anglicized metaphysics could still be discerned. Similarly, Hobbes's frequent visits to France and friendship with Mersenne may have paved the way both for a turning of Cartesian skepticism against itself by posing sense impressions and the memory of these impressions as the fundaments of knowledge, and for the deployment of these fundaments against the Cartesian rationalist solution to skeptical inquiry.

Derrida too is a thinker for whom the "how" of the "how to avoid speaking" is affected by the language of the other, the other who does not speak French. I shall not enter here into an account of the strategies of negation deployed in the ironic discourse of Derrida's comments on Anglo-American analytic philosophy, "Limited Inc."[3] Its ripostes are marked by the difference between two encounters, that of the immediate controversy between Jacques Derrida and John Searle and the traces of the earlier quarrel between Rousseau and Hume never mentioned by Derrida or Searle that resulted in Rousseau's remarkable dialogues *Rousseau, Juge de Jean-Jacques.* Could one not in the spirit of play think of "Limited Inc." as Derrida's *Derrida, Juge de Jean (John Searle) et de Jacques (Jacques Derrida)?*

Consider too, in compliance with his own admonitions, about the non-French mise-en-scène of Derrida's account of how not to speak. "I thus decided not to speak of negativity or of apophatic movements in, for example, the Jewish or Islamic traditions . . . leav[ing] this immense place empty, and above all that which can connect such a name of God with the name of the Place [Jerusalem where the address on negative theology is delivered]" (*LU,* p. 53), Derrida says, putting out of play the double heritage of Jew and Arab, of a Jew born in El Biar outside Algiers, of a double "orientalism" as it were, that should, by right, place the discourse of negation within its "natural" setting. Would not this setting consist of the Mu'tazalite discussion of the not as the problem of a God who wills not to do evil as well as of Philo's account of God's incomprehensibility and his strict interpretation of the Jewish scriptural prohibition against comparing God to lesser beings. Without once resorting to Mu'tazalite sources that reflect the refusal to attribute evil to the divine nature and the Jewish stricture against naming the unnameable, Derrida speaks the discourse of the avoidance of speech through Plato, the Pseudo-Dionysius, and Meister Eckhardt.

Although the question of negation is the "leitmotif" of twentieth-century French philosophy, as Vincent Descombes in his history of recent French thought observes,[4] Derrida, in his discussion of negative theology, remains silent in regard to the rift or breach in its articulation within French philosophy itself. Descombes distinguishes two modes of interpreting negation. In a somewhat oversimplified but suggestive scheme, he argues that French thinkers divide into those who "attribute to non-being the paradoxical ability to present itself," and those who believe it is *we* who "introduce non-being by virtue of the mind's capacity to set itself against what is."[5] With this distinction in mind, it can be argued that privative negation grounded in ontological fullness and reflecting the influence of Neoplatonic Christian thought is represented in the philosophies of Bergson, Marcel, Maritain, Duméry, and the Marxist-Freudian amalgam of Deleuze and Guattari. Negation as lack rooted in subjectivity derives from neo-Kantian and Hegelian philosophy and is expressed in the thought of Sartre, Levinas, Blanchot, Lacan, and, despite significant countercurrents, in Simone Weil.

I hope to show that Derrida, exiled from both of these French textual practices, stations himself neither in ontological plenitude nor subjective lack and that to say no in French may lead one to speak otherwise than within this system of oppositions. To situate the no-saying of Derrida, this no-saying must be placed in conversation with Bergson's account of negation, the most influential case in point of the first type.

BERGSONISM AND METAPHYSICS

Consider as exemplifying the tendency of ontological plenitude, Bergson's view, not in itself as it were, but as refracted in the interpretive light of Deleuze's complex contemporary reading. Deleuze's description of Bergsonian negation manifests itself at three levels: first, Deleuze's isolation of Bergson's treatment of the question of falsity in stating and solving philosophical problems; second his analysis of Bergson's use of the question of nonbeing as an example of a false problem; and finally his consideration of Bergson's analysis of differentiation not as something negative but as a creative process.

According to Deleuze, false problems for Bergson stem from two sources, one bound up with Bergson's understanding of nonbeing, the other with a category mistake (in the Anglo-American sense) in the construction of the problem itself. The second difficulty, that of the false problem, is, Deleuze suggests, "a case of badly analyzed composites that arbitrarily group things that differ

in *kind*."[6] As a case in point Deleuze cites Bergson's analysis of
the intensity of sensations, an issue that is generally framed, Bergson thinks, in inappropriate language. The qualitative nature of
the sensed is analyzed in terms deriving from the world of space,
of mechanism, of that which can be quantified, in this instance
"with the muscular space that corresponds to it, or with the quan-
tity of the physical cause that produces it."[7] To speak of intensity
in terms of "how much" is to misunderstand its character.

Similarly the problem of freedom is often misstated when it is
articulated in spatial terms rather than in terms of duration, or
pure states of consciousness. In consciousness there are successive
states that cannot be distinguished from one another in the sense
that one state is felt as ceasing when the other arises: "Outside us,
mutual externality without succession," or simultaneity; "within
us, succession without mutual externality," Bergson avers.[8] Only
when we grasp ourselves as we are, in terms of time and duration,
are we genuinely free.

The false problem stated in terms of wrongly grasped composites
is the root error of another problem, that of describing nonbeing
as if it were something. Strangely enough, Bergson's analysis an-
ticipates Quine's argument that the language of negation leads to
the positing of what is not simply because we can talk about it,
"the old Platonic riddle of nonbeing, [that] in some sense must be,
otherwise what is it that there is not?"[9] But to see the difference
in thrust between Quine on the one hand and Deleuze and Bergson on the other, it should be recalled that Anglo-American philosophy sweeps away nonbeing in order to limit the ascription of
being to those entities described in mathematical and physicalist
accounts. Bergson, seeking a richer experiential matrix, consigns
such objects, including mathematical objects, to their origin: the
imagined plane of a homogeneous space.

Bergson believes that nonbeing is the result of a judgment made
about existing things, yet nonbeing is affixed to things as if it had
an existence of its own. Bergson, says Deleuze, believes that "the
more is mistaken for the less" and sometimes "the less . . . for the
more."[10] For example, doubt about something we plan to do adds
nothing to the proposed activity but instead reveals a privation or
weakness in the doubter.[11] Deleuze goes on to cite Bergson's statement: "For we feel a divinely created will or thought is too full of
itself, in the immensity of its reality, to have the slightest idea of a
lack of order or a lack of being. To imagine the idea of absolute dis-
order, all the more the possibility of nothingness, would be for it

to say to itself that it might not have existed at all, and that would be a weakness incompatible with its nature, which is force. . . . It is not something more but something less; it is a deficit of the will."[12] Bergson is condemning thinking in terms of degree that results from muddling the separate orders of time as duration and space as mechanism and conflating both of these with an idea of being-in-general that then becomes the foil for nothingness.[13]

Deleuze declares that despite his insistence on differences in kind, Bergson also works from an altogether dissimilar principle, one that enables him to move from dualism to monism.[14] Guided by the concept of expansion (détente) and contraction, the two, matter and duration, can be seen as aspects of one another. Although Deleuze does not say so, it is easy enough to see that if Bergson views negation as privative rather than as what can limit a type of being or oppose one type of being to another, then there is no way of accounting for differences in kind. There is ultimately only a plenum that stretches and shrinks to account for difference. Expansion and contraction, Deleuze suggests, are relative terms: "What is expanded if not the contracted—and what is contracted if not the extended, the expanded. *That is why there is always extensity in our duration and always duration in matter*." "Duration is never contracted enough," he goes on to say, "to be independent of the internal matter where it operates, and of the extension it comes to contract." Duration then is matter contracted and matter duration expanded. Imperceptibly an ontological hierarchy is restored: differences in kind are high on the scale, differences in degree low. This monistic moment, Deleuze argues, "is not without similarity to the One-Whole of the Platonists. All the levels of expansion and contraction coexist in a single Time and form a totality."[15]

But this "monistic moment" is poorly understood unless its deviation from Platonism is grasped. Bergson speaks of this totality as a *virtual* whole, a totality as different from the static plenum of the Neoplatonists as his attack on nonbeing is from Quine's. What Bergson means by virtuality is comprehensible only in terms of his grasp of the essence of life, the élan vital, life itself, a totality that is always in the process of self-differentiation, one that presupposes a prior unity that splits off into the ramified branches of life such as plant and animal or instinct and intelligence.

What is crucial for Bergson is that the virtual character of the whole not be confused with the classical notion of the possible. The idea of possibility, Bergson thinks, is a shadowy imitation of the real: the difference between the concept of the possible and of the real is merely that existence is added on to the possible to construct the real. With possibility, everything is already precut. The idea of possibility can be explained psychologically as a backwards projection of some actuality, an image formed of it based on the real but as antecedent to it. The virtual on the other hand creates as it actualizes and thus accounts for novel forms of life. "It is difference that is primary in the process of actualization— the difference between the virtual from which we begin and the actuals at which we arrive." The lines of differentiation are created in the process of actualization. Deleuze concludes that the reality of the virtual is conceived as "a gigantic memory, a universal cone in which everything coexists with itself, except for the differences of level [themselves virtual and belonging] to a single Time; they coexist in a Unity; they are enclosed in a simplicity; they form the potential parts of a Whole that is itself virtual. They are the *reality of this virtual.*"[16]

While the question cannot be pursued in detail here, it is worth noting that Descombes is not wrong in viewing Deleuze as the heir of Bergsonism. It can be argued without much difficulty that the fundaments of Deleuze's own philosophy, a plane of organization with its multiple structures and layers on the one hand, and a plane of movement and rest, a plane of varying intensities, on the other, is a rearising in social and psychological form of Bergsonian metaphysics.[17]

In sum, to say no is, for Bergsonism, first to decompose false composites, a deconstructive move that establishes the heterogeneity of kinds such as matter and memory or instinct and intelligence. This heterogeneity is supplemented by a second type of negation understood privatively, an ontological thinning of the object, for example, doubt as watered-down conviction rather than as a negative state. Within this scheme there is no strategy for setting off ontologically heterogeneous kinds through the logic of limitation or opposition so that differences cannot be explained. Bergson is almost forced to posit a totality and principles of change, in this case expansion and contraction, that function within the totality to account for the emergence of heterogeneity.

There is already within the Bergsonian-Deleuzian metaphysics a highlighting of succession as repressed by intelligence in its quest for socialization and the mastery of nature, an intelligence driven by a spatialized thinking that requires the halting of time. Bergson and Deleuze resolve this dilemma by positing a double plane:

that of plenitude, whose mode of temporalization is simultaneity, presence, and language, and that of dynamism, whose mode of manifestation is successive and impervious to linguistic articulation. Derrida retains these oppositions, relocating them within a philosophy of textual practice, a revision that will keep the scheme of these functional distributions while altering their field of articulation.

Bergson, Derrida, and the Beyond of Language

Two spatial fields or topoi within the discourse about the avoidance of speech are singled out by Derrida: the *chōra*, or receptacle of Plato's *Timaeus*, in which the intelligible forms are inscribed, and Jerusalem, the place where he happens to be delivering his lecture on the avoidance of speech but also the sacred place imagined in the *Mystical Theology* of the Pseudo-Dionysius. These are the settings, the geographical sites for the localization or the coming into language of what had heretofore remained silent: through the *chōra*, the whole field of unfolding of Plato's metaphysics; through Jerusalem, Derrida's own thoughts about deconstruction as the avoidance of speech as well as Dionysius' reflections on the ineffability of the divine essence. Language (rather than a nondiscursive force or élan as in Bergson) has been singled out as the plane of articulation for the investigation of nonbeing, a language that moves back and forth along the double track from which negative theology emerged: the languages of Athens and Jerusalem.

Derrida compels the language of Greek philosophy to recede to the point where it can no longer speak, to the point where it becomes the nonplace of the *chōra* (literally, receptacle) described in Plato's *Timaeus*, in which the forms themselves are inscribed. Lying beyond the eternity of the forms or the distinction of being and becoming, the *chōra* "precedes" intelligibility. Because it is neither one nor the other, it easily lends itself to appropriation by both the intelligible and sensible worlds and can only be spoken of negatively: "The *khōra* is the atemporality (*l'anachronie*) itself of the spacing; it (a)temporalizes (*anachronise*); it calls forth atemporality, provokes it immutably from the pre-temporal *already* that gives place to every inscription" (*LU*, p. 36). If this is so, the *chōra* of preinscription cannot enter the series of dynamic, disseminative, and deconstructive terms that constitute the Derridean critique of Western metaphysics such as *différance*, the hinge, the supplement, woman, and the like, for these terms depend upon a dynamic temporality of delay and deferral.

Bergson's discussion of Plato and Aristotle in *Creative Evolution* simply restates the received distinctions: being and becoming, form and matter, the sensible and the intelligible, motion and rest, so that one seeks in vain for an interpretation comparable to Derrida's description of the *chōra*. For a more pertinent concept in Bergson, it is useful instead to remember Bergson's critique of Einstein's account of space-time. The multiplicity of times in relativity theory is unified only in a fourth dimension of space, Bergson argues, thus reintroducing a conflation of space and time and creating a false problem in Bergson's sense of the term.[18] This composite forces Bergson to imagine what it would mean to think of a *pure* space. Such a space could not be that of the physical world—physical space is not atemporal—but would be a purely homogeneous space prior to the division into geometrical or mathematical space and physical space: not purely mathematical, for that would not yet be space, and not exclusively physical for matter alone would fail to coincide with mathematical law that expressed its order. Thus Bergson writes in *Creative Evolution*, "The laws of mathematical form will never apply to [physical space] completely. *For that it would have to be pure space and step out of duration*" (emphasis mine).[19] This pure space, motionless, incorporeal, prior to extensity, as described by Bergson occupies the same metaphysical locale, so to speak, as the *chōra* in the *Timaeus* as understood by Derrida.

Turning to the second plane of negative discourse, Jerusalem, Derrida begins by citing his relation to this city as both anterior to the present and as future. The unmentioned site of this relation is the classical Jewish discourse about Jerusalem: the city that is yet to come and to which one is always already obligated. Derrida claims he is never present in Jerusalem but always already "there," there where he will be. I interpret this "already" as inscribed in the *ja* of *jamais*; at the same time the *mais* deriving from the root *aiw* is marked by an always or ever that stretches towards the future. Thus Derrida can say of his promise to speak in Jerusalem, "It is not certain that I am keeping my promise today; nor is it certain that in further delaying, I have nevertheless not already kept it" (*LU*, p. 13).

This refusal of presence by locating the promise in past and future does not exhaust the possibility of the discourse about Jerusalem. Mystical speech relocates the city as Eckhart, cited by Derrida, avers, to a site " 'as near to my soul as the place where I am now' " (*LU*, p. 14). This dislocation is explicated in Derrida's analysis of Dionysius' *Mystical Theology:* there is the place from which the address to the Divine source issues, the place of " 'separa[tion] from the many' " where the speaker who is purified may stand and the place which is not a place to which it is addressed, " 'the place where God is' " (*LU*, p. 22). If God is incorporeal, "the place where God is" might be thought to be nondifferent from God, but this is not so. God and his place are not the same, not because something sensible still clings to place—God's place is, after all, the space of intelligibility—but rather because God transcends intelligibility itself as " 'the presence . . . above the intelligible summits of . . . the most holy places' " (*LU*, p. 22). Yet it is God who liberates the corporeal power of speech, in this case the power of a speech of denial that avoids direct speech.

What is it then that takes place (*ce qui a lieu*), Derrida asks, in this divine nonspace? How does one pass from the first space, from the speaker's initial address to God, to the second, God's own space? The power of speech whose referent, God, remains the ineffable name is what takes place in the space of a language that includes in itself a silence, the name that cannot be pronounced. What comes to pass is not language as such but the language of prayer, the address to God, and the apostrophe, the address to the absent reader. Derrida explains: "[Apostrophe and prayer] from one you to the other, thus weave the *same* text, however heterogeneous they appear. There is a text because of this repetition. . . . The identity of *this* place, and hence of *this* text, and of *its* reader comes from the future of what is promised by the promise. . . . The apophasis is brought into motion—it is initiated . . . —by the event of a revelation which is also a promise" (*LU*, pp. 48–49).

The Place, the Holy of Holies as it were, is the place of writing where God sets down the promise recorded in Scripture. "It is the place only after what will have taken place—according to the time and the history of the future perfect. *The place is an event*" (*LU*, p. 49; emphasis mine). The dynamism of the promise sets in motion what could have been the topos of a static space such as that of Neoplatonism. Revitalized by the introduction of the promise, the topos of Scripture can never be integrated into a totality. The time of the promise is the time I designated earlier as the "referent" of the negative particle *jamais*, the temporalization of never in Derrida's sense of always already: one is, on his view, always already in Jerusalem.

Two conclusions can be drawn from this geographical exercise: first that Jerusalem enters that series of cryptic terms that for Derrida mark the crossing over of time and space: trace, hinge, writing, *différance* and so on; second, these terms, create a temporalized space in which the static plenum of Neoplatonism, of the *Mystical Theology*, is set in motion. This space is, when viewed from a functional perspective, a Bergsonian "plane" where ever-new manifestations of life are created or a Derridean "plane" where texts can never be brought to closure.

LEVINAS, DERRIDA, AND THE PRESENCE OF ABSENCE

Earlier I distinguished two types of nonbeing, ontological fullness, in which privation of being denotes nonbeing, and a lack that is itself hypostatized. It is time to consider Derrida's relation to the latter mode of negation. Derrida remarks that "to speak for nothing is not: not to speak: and above all it is not to speak to no one" (*LU*, p. 6). To speak "for nothing" can mean to speak gratuitously or it can mean to speak on behalf of nothing, of the positivity of nothing as it were. This is the Nothing announced in the discourse of Heidegger: "One could read: *What Is Metaphysics?* as a treatise on negativity. It establishes the basis for negative discourse and negation in the experience of the Nothing which itself 'nothings' (*Das nicht selbst nichtet*). The experience of anguish puts us in relation to a negating (*Nichtung*) which is neither annihilation (*Vernichtung*) nor a negation (*Verneinung*). It reveals to us the strangeness of what is (*das Seiende*) as the wholly other" (*LU*, p. 53).

I shall not enter here into a discussion of Derrida's account of the logic, rhetorical strategies, and historical situation of Heidegger's relation to the question of nonbeing. Instead I shall turn to the second part of the remark cited: to speak of nothing is "above all, not to speak to no one," a comment that points to the connection of the nothing to an addressee. This remark places Derrida into conversation with the philosophy of Levinas, for whom no language exists without an invocation of the other. If, as I argued, the *jamais* is the negative particle governing Derrida's ties to Bergson, *nul* or *nulle* in the sense of "not anyone" is the word of negation that presides over the relation to Levinas and points to the impossibility of a purely monological discourse.

Derrida has commented extensively on Levinas's work in "Violence and Metaphysics" and in "Me voici, Emmanuel Levinas,"

his contribution to a festschrift for Levinas.[20] Thus the place of
the Other in Derrida's account of negative theology need not be
based largely on inference but is governed by an explicit reading
of Levinas's view of alterity.

For Derrida the problematic established by Levinas's philosophy
is how to think without thinking ontologically, how to develop a
thought "that no longer seeks to be a thought of Being and phe-
nomenality," how to stammer, as it were, a prophetic speech that
infiltrates the logos of Greek philosophy. Ontological thinking
cannot work without reducing what is other than itself to a mode
of knowledge or consciousness. Levinas's shift, says Derrida, is an
effort of thinking to free itself from an ontological or transcenden-
tal oppression, that of the Same and the One, from which there is
no egress. A corollary of this interpretation is the idea that metaphysical oppression is the source of "oppression in the world," that
ontology is, at least indirectly, a thinking of war and violence. The
departure from ontology "calls upon the ethical relationship—a
nonviolent relationship to the infinite, as the infinitely other, to
the Other—as the only one capable of opening the space of transcendence and liberating metaphysics." This ethical thinking is an
ungrounded non-ontological thinking "progressing by negations,
and by negation against negation."[21]

Derrida develops the negations of Levinas's thought at two levels, that of ex-cendence and of transcendence. The first level takes
as its starting point the Good beyond being of Platonic metaphysics but departs from ontological and categorial philosophizing
because thinking the Good is projected toward the Other. This is
the aspect of Levinas's work that is stationed at the outermost extreme of philosophical discourse but remains in complicity with
an intraphilosophical language. Such thinking is still problematic
because the metaphor of the Good as the sun that illuminates and
makes visible may draw one back into the framework of ontology.

Beyond ontology, departing from it altogether, is a metaphysics
or ethics governed by the rule of desire. "Metaphysical transcendence," Levinas avers, "is desire," for (in the sense of on behalf of)
an absolutely Other. Unlike need, it cannot find fulfillment in objects of satisfaction but remains an excess, a something more than
what can be "encompassed by a totality." Its object, the Other, is
infinite because always more than can be framed within a concept. Desire belongs to what is most primordial in language, the
dative or the vocative form of address and the most pristine form
of this primordial language, the address to God. The Other is like

God so that "via the passageway of this resemblance the Other can be lifted up toward God" to a discourse *with* God and not about him thus to an a/theological discourse.[22] An infinite distance is maintained between interlocutor and addressee, a stress upon an absolute exteriority that distinguishes Levinas's negation from the protocols of traditional negative theology.

"The complicity of theoretical objectivity and mystical communion will be Levinas' true target," Derrida insists.[23] Although Derrida does not put the matter in this way, the one who cannot be incorporated in thought is not a "someone," a being upon whom an identity can be conferred, but a "not anyone." Derrida's view of the Other in Levinas is, on my reading, governed by the negative particle *nul / nulle,* not as connoting the negation of a generalized Everyman but—to stretch Homer's meaning some—in the sense intended by Odysseus who, when asked to identify himself to the Cyclops, eludes recognition through the ironic self-designation "Nobody." The "I" of Odysseus gives way to a "not anyone" at the same time that his helpless and terrified men are also "not anyone," not the objects of a concept, but those others who issue a direct appeal and by whom he feels commanded.

In Derrida's essay on how to avoid speaking, the account of the Other as the self's interlocutor has been prepared in Derrida's earlier analyses of Levinas. The question of the Other is now raised in a new context, that of the referent of negative theological discourse. If the referent cannot be identified in intraontological speech, what are the "terms" in which an alternative discourse can "manifest" itself? "The possible absence of a referent still beckons," Derrida claims, "if not toward the thing of which one speaks . . . at least toward the other (other than Being) who calls or to whom the speech is addressed—even if it speaks to him only in order to speak, or to say nothing" (*LU,* p. 28). But the speaker does not speak unbidden because there is a call from the Other that precedes speech. Derrida continues in a purely Levinasian idiom: "The most negative discourse . . . preserves a trace of the other. A trace of an event older than it *or* of a 'taking-place' to come" (*LU,* p. 28).

The important point is that negative theology is not an autonomous discourse, does not fall within historical time but belongs rather to the language of command and promise: the speaker is ordered into relation with the Other and promises to obey (*LU,* p. 29). This is precisely the point made by Levinas in his account of prophecy or "pure testimony, pure because prior to all disclosure;

it is subjection to an order before understanding the order. In the recoverable time of reminiscence it is no less paradoxical than a prediction of the future . . . it signifies in the sense in which one says *to mean an order;* it *orders.*"[24]

For Derrida (as for Levinas) the one commanded is responsible for speech, a speech that falls into the prescribed syntactic and semiotic patterns of prayer and apostrophe. Prayer demands that the Other take on the role of addressee by hearing the prayer, a supplication to the Other to "give the promise of His presence" (*LU*, p. 42). The pure supplication of prayer is marked off from encomium, which preserves an element of affirmative speech and opens a way to the hyperessential designations of God in mystical speech. More, the supplicant turns to another addressee in order to lead that other to God without himself turning away from God and thus opening the prospect of a community of negative speech (*LU*, pp. 47–48).

The relation of these planes, that of negation, of demonstrative, and of analytical theological discourse, is the problem addressed by the theology of Dionysius, Eckhart, and other Christian mystics. "The theologian must practise . . . the double inscription of his knowledge. Here Dionysius evokes a double mode of transmission . . . unspeakable, secret, prohibited, reserved or mystical, 'symbolic and initiatory'; on the other hand, philosophic and demonstrative. The critical question evidently becomes: How do these two modes relate to each other? What is the law of their reciprocal translation or of their hierarchy?" (*LU*, p. 24). Is this not the same problematic that Derrida suggests governs Levinas's work when Derrida writes, in "Violence and Metaphysics": "The complicity of theoretical objectivity and mystical communion will be Levinas's true target?"[25] The avoidance of speech in negative theology already occupies the same discursive terrain as the "true target" of Levinas's investigation, the nonspace of the Other who cannot be brought into plenary presence.

Derrida: The Difference between Bergson and Levinas

It is no accident that Derrida comments, albeit briefly and enigmatically, about Bergson in the essay on Levinas. There he remarks: "Negative theology never undertook a discourse with God in the face to face, and breath to breath, of two free speeches. . . . Analogously Bergson had the right to announce the intuition of duration, and to denounce intellectual spatialization, within a language given over to space." Bergson's intent, he continues, is not to save but to destroy the discourse of metaphysics. Because Bergson privileges metaphysical intuition, language is used and abandoned, so that language for Derrida's Bergson is the *ne pas dire* (how not to speak) of a speech lost to metaphysics. "Like negative theology," he says "[Bergson's] philosophy of intuitive communion gave itself the right to travel through philosophical discourse as through a foreign medium."[26]

But when metaphysics is identified with *speech* and when what transcends language is the *Other*, new problems appear: how can language find a point of contact with what is altogether exterior to it? Speech can only maintain the separation between the Other and the discourse of metaphysics, can only posit the Other as providing the warranty for speech without bringing the Other into predicative language. For Levinas the very words that inaugurate the threshold between itself and the Other constitute a language of entrapment and violence. As Derrida astutely observes, in Levinas's eyes "speech is doubtless the first defeat of violence, but paradoxically, violence did not exist before the possibility of speech."[27]

Preserving the sanctity of what lies outside discursive language, the hallowing of the Other that cannot be conceptualized is also integral to Christian negative theology. Here too speech can be viewed as a kind of violence, a weapon to forestall the dissemination of what should remain concealed. Derrida thinks of such language as instrumental, of its ruses and rhetorical strategies as "technical mediations, weapons, at least defensive weapons," to preclude profanation of the "sacred mysteries" (*LU*, p. 24). Such also are the weapons of Derridean deconstructive language which both conceal and reveal the inaccessible "infrastructure" of metaphysics.

In sum, I conclude that Derrida proceeds by way of graded differences in speaking the language of negation. The first marking off of difference is the distinction between deconstructive negation and negation designed to stress the divine perfections, the encomia found in classical Christian mystical texts. This no-saying sets deconstructive "apophatic" discourse apart from the "hyperessential language" designed to stress God's attributes. A second articulation of difference is a function of Derrida's relationship to the problem of negation in recent French thought. This association is not always made explicit and must be brought out by internal textual analysis as is the case in the relation to Bergson. Derridean negation and Bergson's stress on a dynamic and flowing temporalization that cannot be made present both exhibit what I have called the no-saying of *ja-mais*, the *ja* that indicates already, and the *mais* that means always and whose root, *aiw*, signifies ever. No-saying in Derrida is also connected to Levinas's account of the Other, of the "not" of alterity, a not that is explicated as the manner in which the Other eludes totalization.

Derrida is "stationed" between these planes of articulation of the negative, the plane of Bergson's *jamais*, the no that is a critique of present time as spatialized, and that of Levinas's *nul / nulle*, the "not anyone," that repudiates the attempt to conceptualize or totalize the Other. But the matter is more complex still because, in Derrida, Bergsonian negation doubles up on itself: Derridean temporalization does not replicate the dynamism of the pure flow of time nor the spurious present that is spatialized time but is a time that is not time, a not-time that is characterized as always already and as yet to come. Similarly, Levinasian negation in Derrida is not a copy of Levinas's *nulle* in the sense of the nonconceptualizable Other or the I that ceases to be an egocentric self. For Derrida the Other is invoked textually as both inside and outside the text, "captured," as it were, in the marks of writing. Although the no-saying of Derrida is marked by the *jamais* and the *nul / nulle*, it is perhaps best "expressed" by the negative particle *nulle part*, nowhere, or more aptly, to borrow Rilke's phrase, "nowhere without no."

NOTES

1. Jacques Derrida, "How to Avoid Speaking: Denials," in *Languages of the Unsayable: The Play of Negativity in Literature and Literary Theory*, ed. Sanford Budick and Wolfgang Iser (New York: Columbia Univ. Press, 1989), p. 15. Hereafter cited in the text as *LU*.
2. "*Ousia* and *Gramme:* A Footnote in *Being and Time*," in *Phenomenology in Perspective*, ed. F. J. Smith (The Hague: Martinus Nijhoff, 1989), pp. 54–93.
3. "Limited Inc. abc (response to John Searle)," *Glyph* (Baltimore: Johns Hopkins Univ. Press, 1977), 2:172–97.
4. Vincent Descombes, *Modern French Philosophy*, trans. L. Scott-Fox and J. M. Harding (Cambridge: Cambridge Univ. Press, 1980), p. 23.
5. Ibid., p. 24.
6. Gilles Deleuze, *Bergsonism*, trans. Hugh Tomlinson and Barbara Habberjam (New York: Zone Books, 1991), p. 18.
7. Ibid., p. 19.
8. Henri Bergson, *Time and Free Will: An Essay on the Immediate Data of Consciousness*, trans. F. L. Pogson (New York: Macmillan, 1910), p. 227.

9. Willard van Orman Quine, *From a Logical Point of View* (New York: Harper and Row, 1963), pp. 1–2.
10. Deleuze, *Bergsonism*, p. 19.
11. Ibid.
12. Henri Bergson, *The Creative Mind*, trans. Mabelle L. Andison (Westport, Conn.: Greenwood Press, 1946), pp. 72–74; cited in Deleuze, *Bergsonism*, p. 19.
13. Ibid.
14. Deleuze, *Bergsonism*, p. 86.
15. Ibid., pp. 87, 88, 93.
16. Ibid., pp. 97, 100.
17. See Gilles Deleuze and Claire Parnet, *Dialogues*, trans. Hugh Tomlinson and Barbara Habberjam (New York: Columbia Univ. Press, 1987), pp. 90–91, on the relation of the planes to desire. For a discussion of Deleuze as a Neoplatonist see my *Saints and Postmodernism: Revisioning Moral Philosophy* (Chicago: Univ. of Chicago Press, 1990), pp. 192–208.
18. Deleuze, *Bergsonism*, p. 80.
19. Henri Bergson, *Creative Evolution*, trans. Arthur Mitchell (New York: Macmillan, 1944), p. 238.
20. Jacques Derrida, "Violence and Metaphysics," in *Writing and Difference*, ed. Alan Bass (Chicago: Univ. of Chicago Press, 1978), pp. 79–153; idem, "Me voici Emmanuel Levinas," *Textes pour Emmanuel Levinas*, ed. Francois Laruelle (Paris: Galilée, 1980), pp. 21–61.
21. Derrida, *Writing and Difference*, pp. 82–83, 83, 90.
22. Ibid., pp. 92, 93, 108.
23. Ibid., p. 87.
24. Emmanuel Levinas, *Collected Philosophical Papers*, trans. Alphonso Lingis (The Hague: Martinus Nijhoff, 1987), p. 171.
25. Derrida, *Writing and Difference*, p. 87.
26. Ibid., p. 116.
27. Ibid., p. 117.

JANE MARY TRAU

5

MODALISM REVISITED:

Persons and Symbols

THE DIFFICULT and persistent problem of reconciling the views of monotheism with Christian trinitarianism has given rise to many intriguing heresies. Modalism is one that is surprisingly appealing. The attraction of modalism is its insistent intuition that if monotheism is to be retained, Christianity must reconcile the tension between one divine being and three divine forms. How can one, at the same time, be three? However, the apparently important distinction between "mode of existence" and "person," and the seed of Docetism that lingers in its central thesis, prohibits the approval of modalism.

If there remains any salvageable and helpful contribution that modalism can make to Christology, it must evolve after a critical evaluation of its central doctrine.

HISTORICAL BACKGROUND

The Problem

Christian thinkers have long struggled to explain how Jesus, the Son, and the Father can be numerically distinct yet substantially identical; and it is certainly true that the ontology of the Holy Spirit is as problematic as that of Jesus. The discernibility of individuals relies upon their having distinct properties and substance. If there were two or more divine beings, they would have to be discernible; otherwise they would be the same numerically. If two beings are discernible, they must have at least one distinct property, that is, some activity or quality which one has and the other does not.[1] These distinctions imply limitations or boundaries. Thus, if there were more than one divine being, each divine being would be limited in some way. Since an unlimited deity is essential to traditional Christianity (at least until the development of Process theology), there can be only one. This is precisely the tension between monotheism and the doctrine of the Trinity, which clearly states that although there is in fact one divine nature there are three distinct beings. How can we reconcile the fact that there can be only one God, one divine nature, yet three individuals who are not three gods and who participate in that divine nature?

Modalism claims that there is only one God who has three different ways, or modes, of being, and God assumes these modes when appropriate. According to modalism's most notable proponent, the third-century theologian Sabellius (hence the theory is also known as Sabellianism), "The same God, though one in substratum, is transformed on every occasion according to the necessary circumstances, and is spoken of now as Father, and now as Son, and now as Holy Spirit."[2]

The obvious difficulty with modalism is its denial that the Father, the Son, and the Holy Spirit are three distinct individuals, or personae. Modalism insists that persona as individual substance cannot be applied to each member of the Trinity. Mode of existence is used instead of persona precisely because the latter had come to mean much more than mask or mere appearance. In any case, modalism rejected any distinction between the three persons entitled by the Trinity and was thus flatly rejected by the Church. Modalism was heretical specifically because it refused to apply "first *ousia*," or persona, to anyone but the Father.[3] The Latin use of persona with its conceptual link to substance must be clearly differentiated from the twentieth-century usage, which is essentially experiential and emphasizes the human characteristics of freedom and self-awareness.

The Use of Person

Ousia can be translated as "essence" or "substance," and denotes individual being. Aristotle uses "first *ousia*" to indicate an individual or particular being, "an individual substance constituting the common substratum of accidents"; while "second *ousia*" refers to a "common substratum of different individual substances."[4] We can restate this as follows: there is one specific genus of divine being that has three and only three distinct members.

Origen insisted that each member of the Trinity is numerically distinct, a real individual being, or first *ousia*. This distinction is again emphasized by Tertullian through his introduction of the word *person*. Tertullian uses persona "as the already conventionalized Latin equivalent of the Greek *ousia*, in which case it was used by him here in the special sense of 'first *ousia*' or real individual."[5] This description is meant to reinforce the notion that each member of the Trinity is not merely a name for an appearance or a thought, but is a real individual, that is, a numerically distinct and substantive reality.

Tertullian's legalistic use of persona is the core of his doctrine regarding not only the Trinity but also the person of Christ.[6] A person may own one property, such as a parcel of land, jointly with several other persons. They each have a right to that common property. Coincidentally, a person may have title to more than one property, and thus may have the right to several parcels of land. This facet recognizes the independent activity of each person. In this legalistic interpretation of persona and the right to property, each person shares in common property, (here divinity), but each has individual claim to that property. The right to the common substance is shared by each individual, or person.

Certainly Tertullian's legal concept of persons sharing in the ownership of property is at best metaphorical, and at worst fallacious when used to clarify the doctrine of the Trinity. After all, *property* used in the sense of attribute or characteristic is quite different from property in the sense of land. And equally, there is an equivocation in the use of *owner*. The problem of the triune nature of the Christian God remained an enigma. It was within this intellectual maelstrom of faith seeking understanding that modalism arose in the third century A.D. and remained as an intellectual force within Christianity until it was finally officially condemned at the sixth-century synod of Braga. As Pelikan points out, the late date of formal condemnation indicates the persistence of the "intuition it represented."[7]

SALVAGING THE CORE NOTION
Reintroducing Modes of Existence

Let us assume that the philosophical assumption that underlies modalism is correct, that the divine nature can be manifested by only one being. This assumption must be accepted if one is to persist in monotheism. What is novel to the thesis here proposed is a perspective founded in the symbolic nature of all existence. Because God is expressive, all that has being is expressive. This approach to the Trinity commences with the divine nature, manifested by one and only one being that is by nature symbolic. A promising path is offered by Karl Rahner's insights into the ontology of the symbol.

Rahner's theology of the symbol begins with the premise that every thing that is, is expressive: all things reach out of and beyond themselves to others. To be is to transcend oneself and establish relationship with others. This is accomplished only by expression or communication, and the medium that accomplishes this expression is symbol. Symbols are the vehicle by which one being is enabled to express himself or herself to another; symbols are the act of creating relationships with others. Furthermore, the self is revealed to the creator of the symbol as it evolves. Thus the symbol is a vehicle of self-knowledge as well as a means for the self to be known by others. Rahner's insight into the special relationship between symbol and the creator of the symbol is the springboard for a new trinitarian understanding.

Rahner's Theology of the Symbol

Rahner states that "all beings are by their nature symbolic, because they necessarily 'express' themselves in order to maintain their own nature."[8] Any thing that exists expresses itself in order to realize its own nature. These expressions proceed from the being, which is a primordial unity (a first *ousia*). Each expression of the unity or individual originates from within the unity and is not external to it. A genuine expression of self is not an appropriation of another object that is separate from the original unity. Rather, the genuine expression of self must originate from within the self and extend outward. The self is perfected and realized as it creates a plurality of expressions, each one revealing an aspect of the self. At the same time, the self retains its unity, *is* the unity of the pluralities. The self does not become diffuse or fragmented as the pluralities are created. On the contrary, the unity that is self is defined and established as the pluralities evolve: the self emerges as the common source and unity of the pluralities.

The created expression is identifiable as an extension of the original unity and is thus distinguishable from the whole. But it cannot be identified as anything other than an extension of the unity in which it originates. Hence the expression truly *re-presents* the original unity. The original unity is somehow present, though not wholly present, in the expression. An expression that meets this description is, for Rahner, a *genuine symbol* of the original primordial unity.

The symbol participates in and re-presents the reality of the original unity, but is not strictly or numerically identical to the primordial unity—it is individual. It re-presents the reality that is its origin, though does not duplicate it. Thus we can say that the relationship of identity between the original unity and the expression is symbolic.

The ontological status of the genuine symbol is unique and paradoxical, for the symbol is an individual yet is not a first *ousia*. The symbol is individual in the sense that it is distinct from the primordial unity from which it proceeds; it possesses its own identifiable boundaries of existence. Yet it exists only as an extension of a genuine first *ousia*. It is apart but not separate, and hence the ontological paradox. The lack of separation between symbol and creator obtains precisely because the identity of the creator so thoroughly pervades its creation that the meaning and identity of the symbol are lost unless it refers back to the unity from which it proceeds. A symbol loses its own essence, and thus its being, if it separates from the reality it represents. At this point, we can comfortably reintroduce the word *person* to mean the primordial unity that is by nature expressive via symbols, and now can say that symbols are individuals but are not persons.

Any given person has multiple expressions or symbols. The symbols or multiplicities are in fact the way in which the person comes to know self and the medium through which the person is known to others. The more multiplicities known, the better known is the person. Each multiplicity is distinct, but not separate from the unity; and distinct and separate from other multiplicities of the same unity. The agreement between one symbol and another is their individual agreement with the unity from which they proceed. Thus the symbols or multiplicities are related to each other by virtue of their common procession from the primordial unity; at the same time, all multiplicities or symbols are inseparable, though distinguishable from, the primordial unity.

Applicable to the Divine Being, it (the Divine Being) as a primordial unity (first *ousia*) must express itself, and precisely because the nature is divine the expressions of the divine primordial unity will themselves be divine. However, these divine expressions, being (divine) symbols, are not separate from the Divine Being. The philosophical requirement of one divine being manifesting divine nature is thus met. The paradox that immediately emerges is that the Divine Being, though first *ousia*, is also second *ousia*. At the same time, the three symbolic expressions of Divine Being are real individuals but cannot be first *ousiai* if they are symbols: genuine first *ousiai* are not symbols for other first *ousiai*; symbols are the media for expression between first *ousiai*. Furthermore, as symbols of the Divine Being they possess some quality of a second *ousia* but cannot be second *ousia*, for there can be only one divine second *ousia*: God is the one first *ousia* of the divine second *ousia*. If, however, we understand the Trinity as three symbolic expressions of the divine second *ousia*, the ontological merit of the persons of the Trinity is not diminished (they remain divine) and the monotheism of Christian faith is preserved.

Now it might be objected that this thesis reduces the Father, Son, and Holy Spirit to mere signs. A sign differs from a symbol by the very fact that a sign does not make present any reality beyond itself; a sign is taken at face value. A Tillichian illustration of the difference between sign and symbol is a stop sign and a national flag: the meaning of a stop sign is exhausted by its presence, while a nation's flag is much more than fabric and design. The flag points to a reality beyond itself; its meaning is not exhausted by its own presence. If the members of the Trinity were mere signs, their meanings would not transcend themselves. The fact that they do point beyond themselves to the divine ground of their own being counts against their being mere signs; they function as symbols of divine being. But is it acceptable to the Christian that they be "mere symbols" rather than primordial unities or persons themselves?

The force of this objection rests on the intuition that if they are symbols rather than persons, the members of the Trinity would not be themselves divine. Divinity, by its nature, seems to require a first *ousia* ontological status. However, it must be remembered that a genuine symbol proceeds from and makes present the primordial unity of which it is an expression. Thus, the divine nature is present, though not completely and exclusively, in each member of the Trinity; each symbol is itself divine.

A second objection is that the members of the Trinity, as symbols of the Divine Being, are somehow less than *fully* divine since a symbol necessarily is not identical to the unity it represents.

This objection can be met as follows. Each expression of the divine being is fully divine, but the reality of the divine is so great and infinite that it can never be exhausted. The three divine expressions of the divine primordial being are themselves fully divine, for divinity by its nature cannot be limited. But because they are expressions, no member of the Trinity can itself exhaust divine nature. Thus, although each individual is itself divine, no individual is identical to divinity as a nature.

These expressions are not mere names or titles (as monarchianism claims). Rather, the symbolic expressions of the divine being are genuine and identifiable realities. They persist independently of and simultaneously with each other, though not separately from the one primordial unity that is their origin.

A third possible objection is that this thesis could lead to Tri-Adoptionism if it were understood to mean that the three members of the Trinity are all subordinate to the Divine Being. This problem is avoidable if the emphasis on the expressive nature of being is retained. The Divine Being is no more separate from its multiplicities than a human person is from his or hers. An individual cannot be separated from his or her multiplicities, for knowledge and actualization, to self or others, are impossible without the pluralities that perfect them. Conversely, the multiplicities, though unique and clearly discernible one from the other, can in no way be separated from the primordial unity to stand on their own. The unity is not separate from or superior to the multiplicities, for it is realized only through them. The multiplicities are not subordinate to the unity because they are the perfection of the unity.

A fourth possible objection is that the Divine Being, as an underlying primordial unity that expresses itself in the Trinity, is too remote or abstract to have any meaning. It is precisely because of this distance and incomprehensibility that the symbolic expression of the Trinity is comprehensible. If the Divine Being is to be known it must, like any other being that is known to itself and others, express itself. In the absence of self-expression, a being not only cannot be known, but cannot exist.

> And it comes to itself in the measure in which it realizes itself by constituting a plurality. But this means that each being—in as much as it has and realizes being—is itself primarily "symbolic." It expresses itself and possesses itself by doing so. It gives itself away from itself into the "other," and there finds itself in knowledge and love, because it is by constituting the inward "other" that it comes

to (or: from) its self-fulfillment, which is the presupposition or the act of being present to itself in knowledge and love.[9]

The Divine Being, which is the one and only member of the class of things that instantiate divine nature, expresses itself so that it may know itself: self-realization requires expression. The Divine Being is accessible to human beings only insofar as it reveals itself. That self-communication is accomplished precisely through the Trinity. And so, in love, Divinity creates the divine symbols of Creator God, Redeemer Son, and Sanctifier Spirit.

Jesus as Word Incarnate is the perfection of God's self-communication. The human Jesus is the visible and tangible symbol of the Divine Being for human beings. As the historical person Jesus of Nazareth, he is indeed a first *ousia*. However, as a symbolic reality that proceeds directly from the Divine primordial unity, the human being Jesus is more than human. In Jesus, symbolic reality and first *ousia* coincide: he instantiates both ontological realities. This ontological synthesis is the mystery and paradox of Jesus as fully human and fully divine. His full divinity is explained by his symbolic reality, while his full humanity is explained by his material reality. Jesus Christ presents not only the paradox of symbolic reality, but further presents the paradox of being at once symbol (which is not first *ousia*) and at once first *ousia*. This paradox is comprehensible only via the phenomenon of Incarnation.

A further objection to this Rahnerian position is that it threatens the community between the members of the Trinity. This can be overcome by recalling that the creative act of giving from the very depths of self to form a new and deeper expression of self is precisely the essence of love. The symbolic expression as an extension of the person is an Other, that is, a reality distinct from the primordial unity (though not separate). This Other, not to be confused with another primordial unity, is a multiplicity of the expressive self. Thus the symbol as Other, created as an outpouring of self, exists by the fact of love of the primordial unity. Each member of the Trinity is in genuine community with the primordial unity of the Divine Being. Because the Divine Being is love itself, the essence of self-giving and creative expression, each symbol contains that reality within it. It could be inferred from the reification of love in each symbol that community exists as a reality between the symbols themselves. As all multiplicities share in agreement with the unity from which they proceed, so the divine

symbols share in the divine reality as perfect love. This sharing in
the creative and expressive reality of the Divine Being is the basis
for the community amongst the Trinity.

A sixth objection may be that this thesis results in a "qua-
drinity" rather than a trinity; that it adds a fourth member to the
trinity. There are two responses to this objection. First, the thesis
insists that there can be only one being that can instantiate the
divine nature. The three persons, modes, or expressions are equally
divine individuals that are inseparable from the primordial divine
unity. There are not three or four gods, but one divine being with
three separate and durable divine expressions, each of which has
unique and eternal identity, and each coexists with the other. Thus
the thesis based on the theology of the symbol avoids the unitarian
solution of modalism as well as a nominalist reduction (of monarchianism), without introducing a fourth element into the concept
of Divine Being.

The second response to the sixth objection can be made by referring to a comment of Rahner concerning the Greek and Latin
points of Christological departure.

> The latter proceeds from the unity of God's nature (one God in three
> persons), so that the unity of the divine nature is a *presupposition* of
> the whole doctrine of the Trinity; while the former begins with the
> three Persons (three Persons, who are of a single divine nature) or
> better, with the Father, who is the source from which the Son, and
> through the Son the Spirit, proceed, so that the unity and integrity
> of the divine nature is conceptually a *consequence* of the fact that
> the Father communicates his whole nature.[10]

The Latin or scholastic perspective originates in the unity of the
divine nature, while the Greek begins with the three persons and
then explains their unity. From the Greek perspective, one might
want to say that the Father is the unoriginated source, or primordial unity from which the divine symbols of Son and Spirit
proceed.

Rahner states that the unity of the Trinity cannot be the "unicity
of the divine nature which if considered numerically is of itself far
from providing the foundation of the three-fold *unity* in God." He
prefers that the starting point be the unoriginated "God the Father
himself, communicated in the economy of salvation through the
Word in the Spirit."[11] Perhaps the metaphysical or ontological
unicity of the divine nature is too remote to convey the liturgi-

cal and experiential character of the Trinity. However, in terms
of philosophical understanding, the unicity of the divine nature
is no less intellectually attractive than the "god" of St. Thomas
Aquinas' Five Ways or St. Anselm's "that than which no greater
can be thought." Even so, it may be consistent with the thesis
here proposed that we shift from God the Father or Creator as first
expression of Divine Being to God the Father or Creator as the
Divine Being.

As originator or creator, God the Father can be the primordial
unity that then expresses itself in the unique and eternal and
divine Son and Spirit. The parental image confirms the role as
originator that is proper to the primordial unity. The original primordial unity, which is the unoriginated creative source of all else,
may be said to be parent. However, the very act of creation, or
"parenting," is itself an act of expression or self-giving. Thus the
starting point of Father-Creator-Parent presupposes the primordial
unity of divine nature itself. We cannot think of Father without
presuming God or Divine Being.

Besides the logical priority of Divine Being to Father-Creator-
God, Rahner's suggestion should be avoided because it could lead
to subordinationism. If we think of the Father as the primordial
unity that generates the Son and the Spirit as divine expressions,
we cannot escape the assignment of a different ontological status
to the second and third members of the Trinity. That difference
is precisely the assumption to be avoided, that the Father alone
is the divine person. If Father, Son, and Spirit are to be ontologically equal, the Father cannot be the primordial unity that generates Son and Spirit as symbols or expressions. If we are to retain
monotheism and the equality of the Trinity, we must insist that
the Divine Being, as substratum, or second *ousia*, is the primordial unity that is realized and perfected in its multiplicities, those
multiplicities being the three divine, eternal, individual, and coexistent members of the Trinity.[12] The best prospect for a success-
ful application of the theology of the symbol to Christology or
trinitarian dogma must proceed from the primordial unity to the
expression of the unity in the Trinity. Thus, the thesis proposed is
most sympathetic to the Latin or scholastic perspective.

This approach has an important consequence for feminist
thought, although one would not hold the position simply because
of this. Once the primordial unity as God is separated from the
image of Father, and the latter is understood as symbolic expression, a broader understanding of that image is possible. The dy-

namic behind the image is the concept of Creator, or Source of All Being. The image is extremely powerful because it answers two of the ultimate questions of human thought: whence do I come? and why? The gender-neutral image of Loving Creator accurately replaces the first expression of the Trinity without the negative consequences of male imagery of the Divine Being.

The members of the Trinity, as modes of existence, are more precisely modes of expression of the one being of which divine nature can be predicated. This thesis allows the retention of the philosophical claim that there can only exist one divine being, while allowing that this divine being must express itself as must all other beings. In fact, it is because the divine being is expressive that all other beings must be expressive.[13] At the same time, Rahner's theology of the symbol establishes the presence of the unity in its multiplicities, thus allowing the inference that the symbolic expressions of the divine being are also divine. Finally, the theology of the symbol postulates the independent and enduring nature of genuine symbols, thereby allowing this application of Rahner's theory to overcome the central objection to the original formulation of modalism.

CHRISTOLOGICAL IMPLICATIONS

If Jesus Christ is truly human, he had to have a genuine historical and material beginning and end; he could not have enjoyed his human existence prior to his human beginning. If Jesus Christ is fully human and fully divine, then his divine nature could not have preceded his human existence, for such a claim would amount to the belief that Jesus existed as some ghost or spirit, waiting to incarnate or assume a human form. The preexistence of Jesus, however, is a tenet of Johannine theology accepted by the Church and must be squared with his historical beginning. If Jesus did preexist his incarnation, it cannot be as the Jesus who is the human and divine Christ: if Jesus is truly human, he could not have existed as the human *and* divine Jesus until he became human!

The theology of the symbol allows us to say that Jesus always existed as a multiplicity within the divine primordial unity—as a potential multiplicity yet to be expressed until the historical Jesus enters material reality. Because Jesus proceeds from the divine reality, he can be said to have real eternal existence as a multiplicity of that unity before he incarnates. However, it cannot be said that the actual Jesus, who is at once human and divine, exists before he exists as human being.

The human Jesus is the symbol of the divine being for human beings, and it is only as a human being that Jesus can be the primordial sacrament.[14] As Word, the preexistent Jesus is indeed an expressive reality of the divine being, but he cannot be a visible, tangible, and perceptible reality for human beings until the Incarnation. Thus, the Incarnation can be seen as the perfection of the multiplicity that is the Word of God: as primordial sacrament—as the foundation of God's self-communication to humanity—that Word is perfected when it attains visibility and tangibility. Although the history of salvation documents God's self-communication to humanity prior to the Historical reality of Jesus, it could be argued that Jesus is the perfection of that self-communication.[15]

The Word of God, as eternal, independent, divine, and coexistent expression of the divine being can clearly preexist the historical Jesus; after all the Word is eternal. The Hebrew Scriptures testify to the Word of God as immanent presence of God in human history,[16] and this preexistent Word is the Word which becomes flesh, that which is incarnated in Jesus. Thus Jesus, who is Word of God, can be said to have preexistence as Word.

It may be objected that potential existence, rather than actual existence cannot be properly applied to Jesus, or any other divine expression. This is an important objection and can be met by restating preexistence as follows: Jesus *actually* exists as Word until he becomes flesh. The potential status of his preexistence in no way militates against his divinity (which must be unoriginated if it is to be divine) or preexistence, for though he is potentially Jesus he is eternally Word. Thus, Jesus' existence is at once eternal and at once historically originated.

RETAINING USAGE OF *PERSON*

Symbols present an ontological problem: they are individuals but not persons. We immerse ourselves in Mozart's symphonies and thus we come to know the man; we delight in the poetry of Maya Anjelou and experience her; we are awed by the works of Michelangelo and we marvel at the man; we receive the Eucharist and experience the presence of Jesus the Christ. We know each other as colleague, friend, Christian, spouse, cousin; yet none of these modes completely presents the unity of self. Each plurality reveals something of the person, to others and to self, but none gives an exhaustive picture. Nor does the totality of pluralities fully reveal the unity which is self. The ontology of the symbol is thus difficult to grasp because it is paradoxical: it is what it is not. The symbol stands alone but not separate; it is distinct but not wholly different; it is Other but somehow makes present the same reality it is not; it reveals but does so incompletely.

The above investigations might seem to suggest that *person* is an acceptable term for describing the three expressions of the Divine Being that compose the Trinity. After all, the Latin *persona* as used by Origin and Tertullian means "individual thing," and the symbols are individual. However, the theory of symbol requires that the Other or Others are never actually separate substances from the primordial unity in which they are generated. Since the current usage of *person* implies individual and separate substance, *person* cannot describe a genuine symbol but only a primordial unity.

This is precisely why the reference to Father, Son, and Spirit as persons is problematic, for if they are persons they cannot be one. However, if there is only one divine person, the Divine Being, who is expressed as the Creator, Redeemer, and Sanctifier, then the three members of the Trinity can be understood as the three who "are" the one. Indeed, it is through the Trinity that the Divine Being can be known as person to itself and others. We know the Divine Being because we know these self-expressions of the Divine. The Divine communicates itself through the creation of these expressive or symbolic realities; they exist for that purpose.

The contemporary use of *person* relies upon the notion of self-awareness and freedom. The multiple instantiations of human nature by human beings create no conflict between the type of nature and the number of persons. As we have seen, this is precisely the problem with respect to divine nature and the number of divine persons.

This does not mean that the members of the Trinity do not have self-awareness and freedom. Surely they must. Creator God must be free if creation is to have value; and must have self-awareness if there is to be any meaning to the creation of humanity in God's image. Certainly if Jesus is human he must be no less than a human person.[17] But the unique participation of three beings in one divine nature demands a different possibility than the personhood of human beings.

The addition of mode or symbol to the use of person in Christological discourse will eliminate the conceptual tension inherent in the notion of three persons who occupy a space that can only be occupied by one. The necessary caveat is that mode be understood as independent and coexistent; and that symbol not be confused with sign, but understood as divine expression created by the love of the Divine Being. The members of the Trinity as symbol must be understood to be fully divine themselves, and representative to themselves and to humanity of the creative love in which they are grounded. Thus, monotheism is not threatened and the three members of the Trinity remain distinct, independent, and divine.

It need not be feared that the symbolic mode of the members of the Trinity will distance them from humanity. For the very expressive nature of their existence is testimony to their accessibility. The essence of their existence is self-giving or love. Furthermore, the history of revelation and tradition catalogues the historical and material entrance of God, in each mode of expression, into human history in the most intimate of ways.

The desire for a personal and intimate involvement with Creator God, Redeemer Son, and Sanctifier Spirit may require liturgical norms to remain unchanged, for it is difficult to commune with a mode of existence.[18] If the faithful must pray to a personal God, then they may insist upon the concept of person because it conveys an intimacy that is possible with no other entity. Intimacy with persons is far more appealing and feasible than intimacy with modes or symbols. Rahner concedes that although the "ambiguity of the word has increased . . . there is no other word which would really be better, more generally understandable and less exposed to misconceptions. We must therefore continue to use the word, even though we know there is a history behind it that strictly speaking is not altogether suitable to express what is meant and has no great advantages."[19] However, the problems which accompany that usage can be alleviated by struggling with the philosophical restraint that there can be only one divine person, only one God.

If we think of that one God as the primordial unity, and the three persons as unique, eternal, coexistent, and divine expressions of that one divine person, then the unity can be seen as truly perfected through the multiplicities that are the perfection of that unity. The unity cannot itself be known but through the multiplicities: the one is known through the three.

The Trinity cannot be successfully described by the *original* formulation of Modalism, for it would force us to the position that one God has three ways of *being*, and that each of those modes is contingent upon the actions of God at a given time. The lack of permanence and stability reduces these modes of existence to masks or titles. But we can say that one God has three modes of *expression* (in the fullest sense of expression, as genuine symbols);

and that each of these expressions is unique, enduring, coexistent, and divine. At the heart of the notion of creation is the Other which is the result of self-giving. Thus the creative act of the primordial unity does result in an Other, in this case three Others. The inseparability of the Other that is symbol explains the unity of the Trinity.

NOTES

I wish to acknowledge my indebtedness to Professor Frank R. Harrison III, Department of Philosophy, University of Georgia, for his insightful comments and suggestions on several earlier versions of this paper. Helpful remarks were also made by Drs. John O'Grady, Joanne Pierce, and Edward Sunshine, Theology Faculty, Barry University.

1. The identity of indiscernibles is a complex philosophical problem that is beyond the scope of this discussion. Although not all philosophers are in agreement, I proceed from the assumption that separate individuals must have some property that is unique (other than spatiotemporal location). If two entities are indiscernible, they are identical. Two entities cannot be exactly identical, for then there would in fact be only one thing. The nature of the property which is distinct between two things that appear to be identical is a complex and problematic philosophical question.
2. Harry Austryn Wolfson, *The Philosophy of the Church Fathers: Faith, Trinity, Incarnation*, 3d ed., rev. (Cambridge: Harvard Univ. Press, 1970), p. 597.
3. This led to the Modalist claim that the Father suffered on the cross with Jesus, or *as* Jesus, thus earning them the additional name, Patripassians.
4. Wolfson, *Philosophy*, p. 318.
5. Ibid., p. 324.
6. Justo L. Gonzalez, *A History of Christian Thought* (New York and Nashville: Abingdon Press, 1970), 1:183.
7. Jaroslav Pelikan, *The Emergence of the Catholic Tradition (100–600)* (Chicago: Univ. of Chicago Press, 1971), p. 180.
8. Karl Rahner, "Theology of the Symbol," in *A Rahner Reader*, ed. Gerald McCool (New York: Crossroad, 1985), p. 121. I shall not attempt to reconstruct Rahner's entire thesis, but merely apply it to the discussion at hand.
9. Ibid., p. 125.
10. Rahner, "*Theos* in the New Testament," *A Rahner Reader*, pp. 135–36.
11. Rahner, "Remarks on the Treatise 'De Trinitate,'" in *A Rahner Reader*, p. 144.
12. The members of the Trinity are ontologically distinct from other expressions of God, such as creation and creatures, which by their material nature cannot assume the properties of eternal beings.
13. Rahner states ("Theology of the Symbol," p. 122) that the plurality of God—the creation of multiplicities that are the perfection of the unity—necessitates the similar pluralistic nature on finite created beings. Plurality, in juxtaposition to simplicity, does not therefore constitute or imply inferiority.
14. Kenan B. Osborne, *Sacramental Theology: A General Introduction* (Mahwah, N.J.: Paulist Press, 1988), p. 71.
15. Sacramental theology is beyond the scope of this paper, and I do not wish to explore the full import of Jesus as *sacramentum* and *res sacramenti*. My inten-

tion is merely to follow to its logical conclusion the implications of Word and Incarnation as perfection of the primordial unity.

16. Carl A. Volz, *Faith and Practice in the Early Church: Foundations for Contemporary Theology* (Minneapolis: Augsburg, 1983), pp. 13–20.

17. The lack of development in theology of the Spirit prohibits me from applying self-awareness and freedom to the Spirit with any real depth of meaning.

18. Pelikan documents the impact of liturgical language on theology, especially in the evolution of Monarchianism (*Emergence*, p. 181). Volz also mentions the phenomenon of *"lex orandi, lex credendi"* (*Faith and Practice*, p. 22).

19. Rahner, "Remarks on the Treatise 'De Trinitate,'" p. 143.

6

TILLICH AND THE

KYOTO SCHOOL

THIS PAPER continues my explorations of Tillich's relations to Buddhism. In a former paper I argued that Tillich's understanding of the symbol of God required that symbol be conceived as a polarity of being and nonbeing. Far from representing—as in most classical theology—an unequivocal antithesis to nonbeing, the symbol of God in Tillich includes nonbeing as an essential ingredient in the divine creative, providential, and redemptive activity.

This argument, if valid, raises the question of Tillich's relation to Buddhism, at least to those forms of Mahayana Buddhism that posit nothingness (sunyata) as the final ground of reality and of authentic selfhood (suchness). Does Tillich's apparent openness to nonbeing imply, then, that being-itself, or God, is *equivalent* to nothingness? If this is not the case, then how does God, if God be a polarity of being and nonbeing, *differ from* nothingness as understood in Mahayana Buddhism? To begin an answer to these two questions, I have in this paper chosen to compare Tillich's thought with two recent volumes representative of the Kyoto School: Nishitani Keiji's *Religion and Nothingness* and Tanabe Hajime's *Philosophy as Metanoetics.*[1]

This comparison must, unfortunately, presuppose some acquaintance with these two examples of Buddhist philosophy as well as with Tillich; to attempt to elucidate their "systems" as preparation for the comparison would itself require two more papers. Because there are substantial differences, as well as similarities, between the two Buddhists—Nishitani representing the

Zen tradition and Tanabe that of Pure Land, or Amida Buddhism —I shall have to take them up separately and compare each in turn with Tillich. Since, however, they do also represent a common stance over against Tillich, we shall seek as well to uncover wherein that more fundamental difference of both with Tillich may lie. As is evident, this is only a beginning. We will by no means have exhausted the richness of any of these three, and clearly even three such major figures do not begin to represent the wide spectrum of authentic varieties within their respective traditions. In each comparison we shall begin with the many remarkable similarities and then discuss one or two significant differences. I shall try to present the arguments of each fairly, but it should be recognized that my pen weighs more and the ink flows more freely when I come to Tillich—a sign, alas, of the lingering presence of attachment!

NISHITANI AND TILLICH

From one point of view the similarities between Nishitani and Tillich are not surprising. After all, both were in a sense "formed" by the classical German philosophical tradition, and directly influenced by both Nietzsche and Heidegger. This common philosophical background does not, however, account for the similarities that intrigue me, namely, those of *theological* method. For both are primarily theologians: that is, philosophers seeking to express in systematic conceptual terms the religious tradition in which each stands. Both are conscious of the problems in the modern setting of that task, and despite the fact that here there are no common influences, both assay it in remarkably similar terms.

I shall list these briefly without comment. (1) Both develop their interpretation of their respective traditions (Christianity and Buddhism respectively) in strict correlation with modern experience and with the modern interpretation of that experience (i.e., modern science, social science, and philosophy). They begin with our situation in the modern scientific, industrial, and urban world. (2) Both are, however, convinced that true understanding is not reached in the terms set by that cultural situation; on the contrary that situation misunderstands itself, especially the presence of lethal threats to its coherence and meaning. Hence, reality is encountered and understanding appears only "beyond" the limits of modern experience, although it also presents us with a more valid understanding of modern experience (*RN*, 5–6, 9–10, 136, 188–89). (3) Entrance into that deeper understanding is existential,

not speculative in character (RN, 15–16, 18, 106–7, 175). We do
not arrive at this deeper understanding via a process of reflection
or through stages of an argument; we move to it by means only
of an existential journey, a spiritual passage of the self seeking to
find itself. To be sure, philosophical reflection accompanies that
existential passage; but it can neither initiate nor carry it through
to its end. In this sense, then, neither one is a speculative, or metaphysical, philosopher—in which, while reflection may express a
spiritual movement or vision or be accompanied by it, it is the re-
quirements of the argument that impel the movement of thought
forward and carry it to its resolution or end. On the contrary, since
in each an existential passage provides both the momentum and
the direction of thought, both are in method as in aim philosophical theologians.

This point is emphasized even more by the important role in
this "new understanding" provided in each case by the religious
tradition, and its central symbols. (4) For in each case the new
understanding ("the answer") comes through the relevant religious
tradition, and its understanding is structured by the received symbols of that tradition. (5) As a consequence, in both thinkers the
interpretation of modern experience and the interpretation of the
traditional symbols of the tradition are "correlated"; and in both
through this process the interpretation first of modernity and then
of the traditional symbols undergoes a thorough "revision." A new
vision of common modern experience thus results as does a quite
new, and in many ways radical, understanding of the relevant traditional religious symbols. Dogmatic proponents of modernity and
of traditional religion are, therefore, inclined to unite in their dis-
taste for Nishitani and Tillich: "too religious" for the committed
modernist and "too modern" for the orthodox religionist. (6) The
hermeneutics employed in reinterpreting the traditional symbols
is in both cases an existential hermeneutic united with a revised
ontology (e.g., RN, 171–73, 243). A religious symbol is understood (and validated) by uncovering its "meaning for our authentic
being" or for our quest for the real self. The symbol, to be sure,
presents an ontology, but we "know" it and recognize its meaning
for us only when we are simultaneously existing spiritually within
that "world" so presented. "Nihility" to Nishitani is not an objective ontological structure; it is an ontological expression of the
experience of the absolute threat of destructive nonbeing. Without
the existential experience, the symbol neither is known nor possesses any content. Much the same is true for Tillich's symbols:

without existential courage, the power of being which is God is not known. (7) Entrance into this spiritual passage comes through the experience of radical negation, and so the realization of our essential limits: the shock of nonbeing in Tillich and the radical experience of nihility in Nishitani (RN, 19, 21, 16, 93–95, 229). In both, fatedness and freedom are in experience and in analysis so closely intertwined that there is no way our own powers of mind or of spirit can conquer the threat posed here by the negation (RN, 23 ff. and 249). (8) In turn this threatening negation is then in both itself negated: by the power of being correlated (necessarily) with existential courage, and by the negation of nihility and its transformation in nothingness for Nishitani, again necessarily correlated existentially via total nonattachment. The similarity of method illustrated in these eight points is, I think you will agree, astonishing.

Even when Nishitani becomes critical of Christianity—after a number of very flattering remarks—he and Tillich are at one. When Nishitani shows that in the modern situation a personal deity, a personal being "in charge" so to speak, makes vast difficulties for a scientifically interpreted cosmos (RN, 49, 57); when he makes clear that a literal beginning and a literal end no longer fit our view of cosmological process (RN, 208–11); and finally when he argues that theism, the belief in an absolute personal being, leaves no room for human autonomy (RN, 37–40, 66–67)—we can hear Tillich cheering from the sidelines. Nishitani regards these three points as essential to Christianity—as do many Christians; and thus for him they represent criticisms not only of the orthodox tradition but of Christianity itself. Tillich too finds these aspects of the received theological tradition objectionable. He holds, however, that they represent "misinterpretations" of the tradition and thus are revisable; and his theology represents, as we all know, a concerted effort to understand finite being and God its ground so that these three criticisms are in principle eliminated.

In his final criticism of Christianity, however, Nishitani opens up, beyond a momentary agreement with Tillich, a genuine and significant region of difference, and thus he provides a clue to what we are searching for in this comparison. The glory and yet, says Nishitani, the fatal flaw of Christianity is that it is centered on the category of the will: it is, finally, *will* that characterizes God as God: as a will toward justice and toward love; and correspondingly it is on the will of the human that Christianity concentrates, as sinful or as redeemed and loving will (RN, 104). This is the glory of

Christianity because through this emphasis the reality and value
of the human person, and so of community and history, were first
realized. But it is its fatal flaw as well—for thereby the bondage
to self-will can never be transcended. Christians believe that they
transcend self-will, inordinate love of self, by surrendering that
will to God, and that thus the problem of self-will is resolved. But
God's vast will is a projection (onto nothingness) of human self-
will (cf. the influence of Feuerbach); consequently that self-will
must return—and does! In self-surrender to God the believing self
now finds itself called to triumph over the world and so to subordinate all the world to itself in the name of God! (RN, 203–4,
208–9). History hardly belies the validity of Nishitani's well-nigh
mortal critique!

This criticism is fundamental, not only as an essential criticism
of Christianity but as an indicator of Nishitani's understanding of
human reality. Since it is also a criticism that Tillich, after a provi-
sional agreement about heteronomy, thoroughly disputes, we shall
follow it out. Incidentally, the same deep confrontation appears
with regard to time; but this one is just as revealing, and it is the
issue Nishitani had raised. Will here for both is, like temporality,
an essential symbol of relative or finite being, and for Tillich of
course also symbolically of divine being; in the discussion of will,
therefore, we see how each views the powers, the fallibility, the
possibilities, and the ultimate meaning of finitude.

Clearly for Nishitani will is an undialectical category: it stands
inexorably for finitude, and so for this finite reality; and in so
representing a reality, it stands undialectically for attachment; for
self-concern, for use of the Other—be it nature or an other—and
so for exploitation. It is the symbol, therefore, for modern self and
modern world: interested, rational, technical self and a world of
discriminated, defined, mechanized and so exploitable "things"
(RN, 5–6, 48–53, 113, 130–36, 188–89, 226–27, 253, and especially chap. 3). A religion based on will is thus grounded in the
problem besetting existence—desire, and self and world created
by desire—and not in its answer, just as modern scientific, tech-
nological, and industrial culture is established on the problem of
the will to power, not on its resolution. Consequently, the only
answer is the cessation of will, not its transformation. Its attachments (desire) must cease, that is, its attachments to itself, to its
objects, and hence to its projects (and so to purpose in time). With
that the reality and value of world, of the world's projects, of self,
and finally of the self's fulfillment, will dissipate. It is the role of

nihility to administer the "shock" (Tillich's word) that makes this cessation possible: nihility appears amidst the apparently solid and meaningful career of ordinary life as the dark abyss under all this coming and going—and the utter transience, emptiness, pointlessness, and accumulated obligations of that world become visible (*RN*, 23, 40, 55, 88, 101–2, 122, 174, 223). Self and world are thus negated as unreal projections of desire and as, therefore, empty; and they are negated through the negation of will, that is, by the advent of nonattachment and so the cessation of desire (*RN*, 71, 90–106, 123, 188, 257). Once the real unreality and valueless-ness of ordinary reality is understood—once it is seen as samsara—then will itself ceases. And with that cessation, self ceases to be self and world, and nothingness replaces nihility as the negation of the negation and thus as a positive ground.

The final step is the cessation of the desire for salvation, and so for a nirvana that transcends samsara. To understand samsara as nirvana—the hurrying world as nothingness and the self in that world as no-self—is the Mahayana "return." The self as no-self stays in the world but on its "home ground": unrelated in terms of desire, purpose, or project to anything external in the world (*RN*, 70–71, 90, 93–96, 106–7, 124, 250). It is "for itself" and not "for us," internally related to nothing although now externally related to all things (*RN*, 116–18). Thus it has no identity as finite, its cen-ter is nowhere in particular, not even in God, and so it is identical with all else: able to serve in compassion but inwardly utterly "at home in itself" (*RN*, 258 ff.). Nirvana or salvation does not mean leaving the world; but it does entail a cessation of will, of the will's power, of its creative projects, and especially of its binding relationships to others. Here is a real point of disagreement.

For Tillich, as for most Christian theologians, will is a dialecti-cal category: that is, it is to be both affirmed and negated, for it can be the bearer and initiator of both good and of evil—as, clearly, can the finite being of which it is the primary symbol. Theologically, therefore, the will, as is the creature of which it is the center, is good (essential humanity) and yet fallen, in existence, estranged from its true reality as dependent on its ground and so from its true identity and value. As separated from its ground, as autono-mous, will is *curvatus in se*. Its natural self-affirmation, its eros for infinite creativity, and its eros-cum-agape relation to others, thus are transformed. Its self-affirmation becomes an infinite self-concern and its creative eros for value becomes concupiscence, the infinite desire to consume all things; and its agape changes to the

drive towards domination and exploitation. Tillich would say of
Nishitani, as he did of Freud, that Nishitani has correctly analyzed
the will as it appears in existence, but he has overlooked will in
essential humanity and in the new being.

Correspondingly, the appearance of a threatening and yet ultimately healing negativity is for Tillich dialectical in its meaning
for the will. The negative appears in the shock of nonbeing: there
the absolute nonbeing latent within all that is finite—like Nishitani's nihility—reveals itself in and through our finite structure:
our temporality, spatiality, causedness, and vulnerable substan-
tiality, and in the separation and disharmony of the polarities that
constitute our finite being. This "shock" brings to the surface our
ever-present anxiety, the threat to its being and the meaning of its
being that every creature experiences. Unless this accumulating
anxiety can be conquered, self-destruction and despair are near
at hand—so far Tillich is not unlike Nishitani. The answer, however, is, interestingly, not nonattachment, the cessation of will,
but courage, the courage to be a self in the world despite the vul-
nerability of the self and the fragility of the meanings latent in the
world. This courage, of course, is the first evidence or disclosure of
the divine power of being in and through which we are. Of interest
to us, however, is that it restores and supports the will; and in that
restorative action (preservation, as the classical doctrines called it)
it saves the will from a fatal delirium of hubris on the one hand
and a despairing descent into nothingness on the other. Tillich is
here clearly restoring self and world, not dissolving them; the will,
and the finite reality it represents and directs, are being healed and
readied for something further, not quieted down.

This restoration, moreover, continues—both inwardly and out-
wardly. Here the category of the new being must enter as carrying
further the process of healing, restoration, and preparation. The
new being restores the will via courage and refashions it via grace.
Thus now—at least in principle, or fragmentarily—the will is no
longer *curvatus in se*, deluded by hubris and driven by concupiscence. Rather repentant, restored, and so dependent on a power not
its own, its necessary self-affirmation as a self is now balanced by
an openness to self-sacrifice. Its eros is qualified by ultimate concerns, projects in the world, which are yet judged and criticized;
and its drive into the future and toward community is governed by
justice and illumined by agape. As a restored will—a fragmentary
example of essence within existence, "Catholic substance" and
"Protestant Principle"—it participates inwardly in all it does and
in each relation it has, and thus is it an individual in the world;

it unites its dynamic vitalities, precisely its "desire," with the creative forms that reason, that justice, and that agape, envision. And above all it accepts its destiny from the past and gives itself to its projects for the future, uniting the separated sequences of time—in repentance, in commitment and trust, and in self-giving. It is in the world, tied to the world, and yet it points not to itself but to the power and meaning working both within it as a self and within the world as a meaningful process.

As is evident, we are now far from Nishitani: it is the restored self, not a no-self, that relates itself creatively to all else. It is, therefore, attached yet repentant, internally related to all yet free, its vitality lured by creative meanings, and participating in culture and community alike. The creative relations to culture and to history that Tillich envisions for the restored self—for the New Being or the spiritual presence in history—sharply differentiates his view—when we look at it closely—from that of Nishitani.

Clearly also the introduction of a transcendent ground for this restoration, and for this new set of relations to creation as a whole, is not arbitrary: if the will, estranged in itself and helpless, is to be restored and become again creatively active in culture, society, history, and nature, then that inner restoration must be the work of an "Other Power," to use Tanabe's terms, a power of being in the will, an order of meaning in the will's relation to its world, and a confidence in the unity of power and meaning for the future. Implied here is not only the creative power of being but also a transtemporal power and meaning that holds the sequences of time and the vocation of the will together, and holds it in unity for the unfolding process of time as a whole. The healing, restoration, and vocation in history of the will depend on a transcendent even unconditional ground of being and of meaning through which the will becomes what it essentially is. Consequently God as the universal and unconditional power of being and of meaning, God as the unity of creative providence and spiritual fulfillment, Alpha and Omega, is at once entailed. Nothingness could not do this divine work; and thus is Tillich, despite his concern for the creative role of nonbeing, not yet a Zen Buddhist! The crucial role of the symbols of creation, of providence, and above all of being or being-itself in Tillich's thought become visible when we compare that thought with Nishitani's.

When we turn to Tanabe Hajime, the relation to Tillich shifts sharply, showing how varied are the possible sets of relations among Buddhists and Christians. If anything, the similarities are greater and more surprising. (1) Tanabe's thought arises directly out of his own social and historical situation, in his experience of himself as "cowardly" and as a "failure" as a philosopher within the imperial, totalitarian, and yet suicidal character of Japan in 1943–45. He found he could not speak as he should, and he despaired. Out of this experience of breakdown, helplessness, and guilt came the awareness of Other Power and of renewal—and his philosophy as metanoesis was born (PM, Preface, il–li). This is, if anything, more existentially and historically centered than Tillich's own experiences in World War I and in the Religious Socialist movement. (2) The negativity that becomes the agent of disclosure is here, therefore, much sharper and more personal than in Nishitani. It represents, for all its historical locus, a personal failure, an experience of personal bondage: of reason, of courage, of moral worth (PM, 26, 47, 112, 144) Tanabe would understand well and second, therefore, Tillich's emphasis on justification by faith, on the wonder of being accepted though unacceptable. The fundamental paradigm for "religion" for Tanabe is, therefore, a series of personal crises very similar to those of Pauline and Reformation piety: action leading to breakdown, self-criticism and repentance (zange), faith and then (interestingly), the latter culminating again in witness or action, action in the world (PM, 82).[2]

(3) It is in this sequence of experienced stages (a sequence Tanabe calls "metanoesis"), and only here, that awareness of Other Power arises (PM, 8–12, 37, 44, 52–55, 66–73, 85–90, 126, 161–62). Without serious action accompanied by the breakdown of action, that is without the initiating self-power as an ultimate concern, no sign of Other Power appears (PM, 17, 155); without Other Power, on the other hand, self-power disintegrates and cannot possibly fulfill itself (PM, 171–73). Knowledge of the absolute is thus "the self-consciousness of action-faith" (PM, 86). This represents, therefore, a radical criticism of Nishitani's view: in that view, within which there is no need of Other Power, there is, says Tanabe, no radical critique of the self, no real negation of self-power, and hence no real renewal. For Tillich, too, experience of the divine power of being arises in and through the negation of our own being, and the assurance of divine grace (new being) arises in and through the breakdown of our autonomous intellectual and moral efforts. As in Kierkegaard, the religious arises not over against autonomy but through it, only when the rational and the ethical "ways" have been seriously tried and then broken down.

As this last point indicates, we have in Tanabe's thought the most explicit and elegant—along with that of Tillich—exposition and defense in our time of the concept of "theonomy"—if I may use Tillich's name for it. And Tanabe is very conscious of this—though not of his colleagues in Germany and in the United States! For he argues explicitly and repeatedly for precisely the union of autonomous action and divine presence that Tillich labels theonomy (*PM*, li, 7, 14, 27, 66–71, 86, 170–71, 175). Jiriki is, says Tanabe, self-power, the serious effort to express and to fulfill one's rational and moral powers; without this effort (as in some forms of the Pure Land) Other Power is empty and useless (Tanabe's form of the Tillichian heteronomy). Tariki is Other Power: without this active presence in and through a collapsed jiriki, self-power either deludes itself (radical autonomy) or dies in despair. Thus the formula "jiriki is tariki" or "jiriki qua tariki" represents the most fundamental expression of Tanabe's philosophical theology. Only through Other Power are reason and the moral will renewed; and yet only through the serious efforts of autonomous reason and morality does this process of renewal take place. It is this sequence of autonomous breakdown, active presence of Other Power, and union of the two in further action that Tanabe terms action—zange—faith-action, or, as noted, "metanoesis." For, again remarkably similar, as we have seen, to Tillich, this sequence, arising out of action in the world, must issue into further, renewed action in the world; Other Power is thus the principle not only of the renewal of the self but of the renewal of the social context of the self as well.[3] And it is this process that Tanabe also labels "mediation" (note the Hegelian background): mediation is the active presence of Other Power in and through relative being, a presence that is intrinsic to relative being on the one hand, just as the media or vehicles represented by relative beings are intrinsic to the presence and action of Other Power on the other. No clearer exposition of theonomy could be given; if anything, even more explicit than that of the master, Tillich himself!

The enthralling convergence, especially on the issue of theonomy, of these two thinkers, from disparate traditions and quite unknown to each other, leads us to wonder how in fact they do differ. Interestingly, it is when each describes to us the character of Other Power, that the latent distinctions between the Christian tilting toward Buddhism and the Buddhist leaning in a Christian direction become visible. For the major argument carried on throughout Tanabe's book—besides the emphasis on theonomy—is that this theonomy is possible only if the Other Power be nothingness and not being (*PM*, 88).

Tanabe's arguments are formidable; they echo not only other

Buddhist philosophers (e.g., Nishitani and Abe) but also antitheistic Western philosophers such as Hegel and Feuerbach. If Other Power be absolute being, says Tanabe, then the freedom and autonomy, the genuine self-power of jiriki—both in the ethical stage preparatory to zange and the ethical action that is its fruit—are sacrificed. That is, if, on the one hand, absolute being be immanent within the relative beings (surely he has Hegel, possibly Spinoza in mind), then it swallows them up as the positive infinite power within their relative power; it becomes the center replacing their diverse centers, and individuality as well as autonomy have vanished. If, on the other hand, in order to avoid this "pantheistic" submergence of the particular, absolute being is distinct from relative being, then absolute being is "over against" each particular. In that case it is either no longer absolute and so no longer the ground of the particular (is he referring here to Whitehead?), or if it is still absolute, it becomes a heteronomous enemy to autonomy, as all Buddhists conceive to be the case in traditional Christian theology (*PM*, 101–2, 271–72). Almost every good argument in modern philosophical theology has, now from a Buddhist perspective, been repeated or implied here!

As a result of these impressive arguments, Tanabe concludes that only if Other Power be nothingness can theonomy be possible. The self cannot die and yet live again without Other Power, but it cannot truly live as an autonomous self unless "room" is made for it, unless Other Power "steps back," unless Other Power represents no self-center, no permanent substance, no program, no being of its own—for in all these cases it becomes a carnivorous absolute. Only as nothingness are the transcendence of the other and the freedom of the relative retained. There can be no genuine freedom of the particular and the relative, no real openness of the future, unless the Other Power in things is nothingness and not itself an autonomous, free absolute being. In nothingness there is no distinct, absolute center, no continuing identity, no permanent substance; there is only the self-effacing presence of absolute nothingness, the absolute principle of mediation and of nothing else. Thus is the autonomous center of each particular both transcended and preserved. Since there is no one center, there can be genuine diversity of centers, and the self can in nothingness be itself and be all selves at once. Through the nothingness of the divine, therefore, the selflessness as well as the freedom of the renewed self are made possible. Tanabe's theonomy and also his emphasis on action in the world seem thoroughly grounded in the category of divine nothingness. This is heady stuff, especially for a theonomist and historically centered activist; what would or could Tillich say?

Tillich first of all would insist that being-itself, as he understood it, was a dialectical category, much as is nothingness to the Buddhist. It is not just referent to the finite, standing for a substance with an identity and self-affirmation, and thus opposed to another's autonomy and identity—as almost every Buddhist assumes it to be; in fact Tillich inveighs against this understanding of God—as a being—throughout his works. Being is thus for him at least a close relative of nothingness insofar as being-itself has for him a theonomous meaning. God as the power of being and the ground of meaning or fulfillment—and that is the definition of God here—is essentially the ground of the being of finite beings and the principle of their meaning and fulfillment. For Tillich no other God is experienced or known. The aseity, unconditionedness, and spiritual character of God appear only in the experience of God as the power of our being and the ground of our meaning. This is, therefore, essentially a dialectical concept affirming and denying at once the absoluteness and the immanence of God, and the absoluteness and the relativity of God. Thus being creates by grounding the self-constitution of others; it preserves and directs by giving to them their self-constituting autonomous being and their self-fulfilling ultimate concerns; and it fulfills, through the renewal of their being and the establishment of a realm of autonomous yet participating beings, the kingdom. At no point is God, so conceived, either an absolute that swallows up and so takes into itself the autonomy of creatures; nor is it an absolute set heteronomously over against them and thus destroying them.

As I have argued elsewhere, this theonomous concept of being itself requires that being here be dialectically related to nonbeing, that God be viewed as a polarity of being and nonbeing. Thus is God enabled, in effect, to function as both being and as nothingness, as Tanabe's sharp arguments—as well as those of Nishitani and Abe—require. If the divine be the ground of change, of natural, historical, and personal process, the living God—to use Tillich's category; if God be an active participant in the world's changes, its victories, and its sufferings, as well as an individual over against the world; and now if God be the theonomous ground of the autonomy, freedom, and creativity of relative beings and of their common history, then, on all these counts, nonbeing is in Tillich's thought as crucial to the reality of God as is being.

Tillich might, if he were feeling his oats, go on a bit further. As our analysis of his thought in distinction from that of Nishitani reveals, centrol to the concept of the restored self, and so a self active creatively, in its social and cultural context, in its relation to others in community, and thus in future time is the positive presence of being within both self and Other Power. Necessary to this role of a self in the world is first (1) self-affirmation (courage), (2) dedication to relevant forms, and (3) commitment to or eros for an ultimate concern on the one hand and for community on the other; (4) norms for self-criticism and self-guidance, and (5) confidence in the future fulfillment of meaning. Here, as we noted, Other Power conceived thus positively as being makes possible the transformation of self-concern into self-affirmation, desire into eros, arbitrary goals into essential ones, meaninglessness into confidence and hope. All this is necessary for creative yet healed action in the world, and all this implies a positive as well as a negative character or role to being, to finite being, and hence to the unconditional being of the absolute ground. God here is creative providence, Logos, and reuniting spirit, all positive characteristics of being. Thus in considering the restoration and renewal of the self and community, the "being side" of the polarity that is God is brought into prominence as, in our more recent discussion of theonomy, its "nonbeing side" was emphasized. If, therefore, Tanabe wishes as he does to stress the restoration of the self into action in the world, he needs to admit as much "being" in his concept of nothingness, as Tillich, in order to be theonomous, needs to inject "nonbeing" into his symbol of God.

That there is both a rich vein of new thoughts to be mined and also much more work to be done in understanding and interpreting the implications of theological dialogue between these two traditions, this paper has, I hope, shown. For example, Tanabe insists that Other Power is nothing more than its action of mediation, so that absolute and relative being are here strictly correlational, the infinite nothingness depending as much on the finite as the latter does on the former (*PM*, 19–20, 118, 183, 272). This raises the intriguing question, Does being-itself for Tillich depend in this essential way on finite being, or is it in some further sense *a se;* and if so, in what further sense? Certainly Tillich would, like Schleiermacher, hesitate to speak of God in God's self, *a se,* independent of creation and of creatures, God as eternally self-sufficient, as did the orthodox tradition. Yet equally certainly, as I see it, he would shy away from Tanabe's explicit affirmation of a symmetrical correlation between infinity and finitude, a symmetrical dependence of the divine ground on its creatures equivalent to their dependence on the divine ground.

I leave this tantalizing question for the moment. Here Tanabe remains Buddhist: the divine principle represents nothingness and little else, a nothingness that flows into and through the relative, the "medium" of the relative, as water is essential to waves, that of which ordinary things are "masks"—to use two of Nishitani's images. Tillich, as we have seen, wishes to say much more than this of the divine ground. And more he must say if his understanding of finitude, of society, and of history is to be as dialectical—and therefore as positive—as it is. Paradoxically, a God who is the source and fulfillment of creation, as well as a negation of its estranged actuality, must itself represent a dialectical polarity of being and nonbeing—neither absolute being nor absolute nothingness.

NOTES

1. Nishitani Keiji, *Religion and Nothingness*, trans. Jan Van Bragt (Berkeley and Los Angeles: Univ. of California Press, 1982); Tanabe Hajime, *Philosophy as Metanoetics*, trans. Yoshinori Takeuchi (Berkeley and Los Angeles: Univ. of California Press, 1986). Hereafter cited in text as, respectively, *RN* and *PM*. For the author's more extensive study of these two volumes, see the volume in honor of Professor Nishitani, edited by Professor Taigetsu Unno (forthcoming) and a review article on Tanabe's book appearing in *Journal of Religion* (April 1988).
2. Perhaps most astounding of all is that in his explication of this strikingly Pauline, Reformation, and neo-Reformation form of piety and of philosophical theology, Tanabe makes no reference at all to Paul, to any Reformation writer, or to any dialectical theologian: apparently only Kierkegaard from the Christian side exerted any influence on him. In describing this predicament, Tanabe uses Kant's label "radical evil"—but clearly his meaning is closer to Reformation interpretations of evil than to that of Kant.
3. There being unfortunately as yet no translation of Tanabe's volume on social ethics, *The Logic of Species*, I cannot comment further on this topic except to point out that he does have a philosophical-theological "theory" on this matter.

7

NEGATION IN MAHAYANA BUDDHISM AND IN TILLICH:

A Buddhist View of "The Significance of the History of Religions for the Systematic Theologian"

In his final lecture, "The Significance of the History of Religions for the Systematic Theologian," Paul Tillich clearly expressed a hope to write a new *Systematic Theology* in dialogue with the whole history of religion. Toward the end of that lecture he stated: "My own *Systematic Theology* was written before these seminars [joint seminars with Mircea Eliade] and had another intention, namely, the apologetic discussion against and with the secular. Its purpose was the discussion or the answering of questions coming from the scientific and philosophical criticism of Christianity. But perhaps we need a longer, more intensive period of interpenetration of systematic theological study and religious historical studies."[1]

An interest in history of religions was not new. It went back to his student days. As Mircea Eliade stated in his tribute to Tillich, "His old interest in History of Religions was reawakened and increased by his voyage to Japan and his encounter with Buddhist and Shinto priests and scholars. The impact of his visit on Tillich's entire life and thought was tremendous. . . . He was impressed and moved by the Shintoist, cosmic type of religion and by the Buddhist and Zen schools." (FR, 31–32).

As a member of the welcoming committee when Paul Tillich visited Kyoto in 1960, I was able to witness in part his encounter with Japanese religions. Tillich's own reflections on his experience in Japan are found in his book Christianity and the Encounter of the World Religions.[2] But as Eliade pointed out in his tribute, Tillich's "profound experience [in Japan], simultaneously religious and cultural, was only partially expressed" in that book (FR, 32). It was through his joint seminar with Mircea Eliade at the Divinity School of Chicago in 1964 that Tillich became deeply attracted by the non-Christian religions and was inspired to develop a new Systematic Theology in dialogue with the history of religions. In his final lecture, "The Significance of the History of Religions for the Systematic Theologian," we can see his provocative and dynamic ideas on the subject in their full scale and depth.

As Jerald C. Brauer wrote in his Editor's Preface to The Future of Religions: "The lecture . . . proved to be one of his most tightly packed and comprehensive lectures of recent years." It includes discussions which are so tightly condensed that it is not always easy (for me at least) to grasp his exact meaning. In the following I would like to examine his final lecture and make some comments from a Buddhist point of view.

I

Tillich rejects the orthodox attitude that dismisses all religions other than Christianity as false, and rejects also a theology of the secular that posits a theology without theos. The former, represented in our century by Karl Barth, absolutizes one's own religion as the only true revelation and regards other religions as futile human attempts to reach God. To this attitude the history of religions has no positive significance. On the other hand, the latter, exemplified by the so-called theology-without-God language, often absolutizes the secular and tries to absorb the sacred by the secular.

Therefore Tillich insists that "as theologians, we have to break through two barriers against a free approach to the history of religions: the orthodox-exclusive one and the secular-rejective one" (FR, 83).

In this regard, I see a parallel of sorts between Tillich's approach and the approach of Mahayana Buddhism. This parallel can be found particularly between their approaches to the history of religions. Mahayana Buddhism criticizes as too narrow Theravada Buddhism, which tends to deify the historical Buddha as the supreme enlightened One beyond human being and regards nirvana as the ultimate goal of Buddhist life. Unlike Theravada Buddhism, Mahayana Buddhism insists on the possibility or even the actuality of attaining Buddhahood for every one of us and emphasizes the dynamic identity of samsara and nirvana. This attitude of Mahayana Buddhism may be regarded as the rejection of the orthodox-exclusive attitude. On the other hand, the Mahayana attitude may also be considered as rejecting the secular-rejective attitude. Its emphasis on the identity of samsara and nirvana does not indicate the absolutization of the secular realm of samsara but, on the contrary, the complete negation of samsara, a negation accompanied by the complete negation of the sacred realm of nirvana. One can see this double negation of samsara and nirvana in a Mahayana admonition: "One should not abide in samsara in order to awaken to wisdom: one should not abide in nirvana in order to fulfill compassion." Accordingly, one may say that both Tillich and Mahayana Buddhism seek to overcome the two barriers against a free approach to the history of religions: the orthodox-exclusive one and the secular-rejective one.

What, then, is Tillich's approach to the history of religion? At one point in his lecture, Tillich states: "My approach is dynamic-typological. There is no progressive development which goes on and on, but there are elements in the experience of the Holy which are always there, if the Holy is experienced" (FR, 86).

With the idea of dynamic typology, Tillich clearly rejects Hegel's construction of the history of religions, calling it a one-directed dialectics in which the past of the history of religions loses its meaning: "For Hegel [for instance] the Indian religions are long, long past, long ago finished, and have no contemporary meaning" (FR, 86).

Instead, his dynamic typology acknowledges a universal religious basis that is the sacramental basis of all religions. The Holy is experienced here and now within everything finite and particular. But in religious experience there is also a critical element that resists the demonization of the sacramental, as well as an ethical or prophetic element, the element of "ought to be." Tillich calls the unity of these three elements, sacramental, critical, and ethical, in a religion "The Religion of the Concrete Spirit" and states, "The inner aim [or telos] of the history of religions is to become a 'Religion of the Concrete Spirit'" (FR, 87, 88). The unity of the above three elements gives the history of religions its dynamic character. The Religion of the Concrete Spirit, however, is not a matter of the future, but "appears everywhere [fragmentarily] in the struggle against the demonic resistance of the sacramental basis and the demonic and secularistic distortion of the critics of the sacramental basis. "We can see the whole history of religions in this sense as a fight for the Religion of the Concrete Spirit, a fight of God against religion within religion. And this phrase, the fight of God within religion against religion, could become the key for understanding the otherwise extremely chaotic, or at least seemingly chaotic, history of religions" (FR, 88).

Here we see the crucial point of Tillich's understanding of the history of religions.

II

Tillich then raises a question as to "how these dynamics of the history of religions are related to the relationship of the religious and the secular" (FR, 89). To Tillich the Holy is not only open to demonization but also to secularization. He states, "These two, demonization and secularization, are related to each other, insofar as secularization is the most radical form of de-demonization" (FR, 89).

The Holy is open to demonization because, once it becomes dominant, it elevates something particular, such as symbols, rites, or institutions, to the ultimate itself. The Holy must be open to the use of the secular as a critical tool against itself.

On the other hand, the Holy is also open to secular, rational and critical movement. The rational necessarily judges the irrationality of the Holy and thus "the Holy becomes slowly the morally good, or the philosophically true" (FR, 90) and ultimately the rational eliminates the religious dimension altogether. However, when the secular fights against the domination by the Holy, it becomes empty and cannot live by itself. Tillich was well aware of this dynamic dimension of the sacred and the secular in the religious experience and emphasizes "the Religion of the Concrete Spirit" as the telos of the history of religions and "Dynamic typology" as the most adequate approach for the theology of the history of religions.

In his book *Christianity and the Encounter of the World Religions*, Tillich talks about the positive relation of Protestantism to the secular realm: "[It is] due the Protestant principle that the sacred sphere is not nearer to the Ultimate than the secular sphere. It denies that either of them has a greater claim to grace than the other: both are infinitely distant from and infinitely near to the Divine. This stems from the fact that Protestantism was largely a lay movement."[3]

If this is the case, the Protestant principle is strikingly similar to the principle of Mahayana Buddhism. As I mentioned earlier, Mahayana Buddhism emphasizes that "one should not abide in samsara in order to awaken to wisdom: One should not abide in nirvana in order to fulfil compassion." It is necessary for a Buddhist to overcome the attachment to the secular realm of samsara and attain nirvana through awakening to wisdom. As Tillich rightly points out, nirvana is the telos of Buddhist life.[4] But, however important nirvana may be, if one simply remains in nirvana one cannot be said to be completely free from attachment and selfishness, since by abiding in nirvana, enjoying one's own wisdom and salvation, one may forget the suffering of one's fellow beings still involved in the flux of samsara. In order to be completely free from attachment and selfishness and to awaken to one's true Self which is identical with the true Self of all others, one must not abide in nirvana and return to the realm of samsara; that is, one must overcome the attachment to nirvana and identify oneself with suffering fellow beings. It is this that constitutes the fulfillment of compassion.

Unlike Theravada Buddhism, Mahayana Buddhism characteristically emphasizes the overcoming of the sacred realm of nirvana by saying, "in order to fulfill compassion one should not abide in nirvana." In Mahayana Buddhism, both attachment to the secular realm of samsara and attachment to the sacred realm of nirvana must be overcome, and that which is neither samsara nor nirvana, that which is neither secular nor sacred, must be fully realized. This is the realization of sunyata, which is often translated as "emptiness."

But sunyata is not a nihilistic emptiness; it is a dynamic fullness. For sunyata is realized only through the double negation of samsara and nirvana. This implies that one must move freely from samsara to nirvana, from nirvana to samsara without attaching to either. This dynamic free movement between samsara and nirvana, between the secular and the sacred, is nirvana in the true Mahayanic sense. Sunyata is simply another term for nirvana in this dynamic sense. This is the reason that Mahayana Buddhism, based on the realization of sunyata, emphasizes that "samsara as it is, is nirvana; nirvana as it is, is samsara." The ultimate in Mahayana Buddhism is sunyata as a dynamic fullness that is both samsara and nirvana and neither samsara nor nirvana at one and the same time.

I would like to call sunyata in this dynamic sense the "Mahayana principle." It is strikingly similar to Tillich's Protestant principle in which "the sacred sphere is not nearer to the Ultimate than the secular sphere. It denies that either of them has a greater claim to grace than the other: both are infinitely distant from and infinitely near to the Divine." The Mahayana principle may be traced to the fact that, like Protestantism, Mahayana Buddhism was largely a lay movement.

III

I am not, however, sure that Tillich's Protestant principle and my Mahayana principle are exactly the same. Rather, I detect a very subtle but essential difference between them. And this difference, it seems to me, entails a different approach to the history of religions between Christianity, as understood by Tillich, and Buddhism, as I understand it.

In both Tillich and Mahayana Buddhism the secular and the sacred are understood to be dynamically identical. In Mahayana Buddhism, however, this dynamic identity is realized only through the realization of sunyata (emptiness), which is realized by the double negation of the secular and the sacred. Since this double negation is not partial but complete and thoroughgoing, it is at the same time a double affirmation. That is to say, negation of negation is nothing but affirmation of affirmation; absolute negation is itself absolute affirmation. And without the realization of absolute negation there can be no realization of absolute affirmation. These statements should not, however, be taken objectively or conceptually, as they do not simply indicate a logical problem, but rather an existential and religious self-realization that can be grasped only in a nonobjective manner. To return to our original issue, in the realization of absolute negation qua absolute affirmation, the secular as it is, is sacred; the sacred as it is, is the secular. As I mentioned shortly before, this dynamic identity is possible only through the realization of sunyata. Although Tillich talks about a similar dynamic identity between the secular and the sacred in terms of the Protestant principle, in my point of view, the realization of sunyata is lacking. For Tillich, the Ultimate is God, not sunyata.

I am not concerned now with the terms or concepts themselves, rather with the reality behind them.

Tillich's notion of God is very different from the traditional theistic notion of God. To him God is the ground of being and the infinite power of being that conquers nonbeing. God is viewed as a polarity of being and nonbeing. However, Tillich's notion of mutually dependent polarity of being and nonbeing is not a thoroughgoing and perfect one. To Tillich being and nonbeing, though consisting of a polarity, do not represent a symmetrical correlation. This we can see from statements he makes in *Systematic Theology*. "Being precedes nonbeing in ontological validity as the word 'nonbeing' itself indicates." Elsewhere he says "being embraces itself and nonbeing" while "nonbeing is dependent on the being it negates."[5] If in Tillich God as the Ultimate is understood as being itself or the ground of being on the presupposition of an asymmetrical polarity of being and nonbeing, the identity of the secular and the sacred must be said to lack sufficient dynamic force to enable it to reach *complete* fulfillment of the Protestant principle where "the sacred sphere is not nearer to the Ultimate than the secular sphere." It must be said to lack enough dynamic force to fully realize "a mutual judging" between Christianity and secularism "which opens the way for a fair valuation of the encountered religions and quasi religions."[6]

On the other hand, if the Ultimate is understood, not as God, but as sunyata, the dynamic identity between the secular and the sacred is fully and thoroughly realized. For sunyata is not being-itself realized on the presupposition of the asymmetrical polarity of being and nonbeing; it is absolute nothingness (or absolute negation qua absolute affirmation) which is realized by overcoming the symmetrical polarity of being and nothingness (I use the term *nothingness* as a stronger form than *nonbeing*) in that sunyata is neither being nor nothingness and yet both being and nothingness.[7]

In the realization of sunyata, Tillich's "Religion of the Concrete Spirit" as the telos of the history of religions is fully realized and we can see the whole history of religions as a fight for the Religion of the Concrete Spirit; however, not as a fight of God against religion within religion, as Tillich suggests (*FR*, 88), but as a fight of sunyata against religion within religion. That this is the case in Buddhism, particularly in Mahayana Buddhism, is seen by the previously mentioned Mahayana admonition: "One should not abide in nirvana, one should not abide in samsara," as well as by other emphasis in Mahayana Buddhist scriptures. We read, for instance, that "all the trees, grasses, and lands attain Buddhahood" and that "the sounds of the streams are Buddha's speech: The shapes of the mountains are Buddha's body." These phrases do not, as is sometimes thought, indicate nature mysticism. Nature mysticism is lacking in the realization of sunyata, emptiness, which is the essential ground of these Mahayana statements. Such secular entities as trees, lands, streams, and mountains are nonsubstantial and empty, without any enduring nature and, precisely because they are so, they are dynamically identical with the sacred. Or we can say the same thing from the opposite side, that since the Buddhist Ultimate is sunyata, nonsubstantial emptiness, it can penetrate or be identical with trees, lands, streams, and mountains.

Quoting Bonhoeffer and other contemporary theologians Tillich states: "[According to them] Christianity must become secular, and God is present in what we do as citizens, as creative artists, as friends, as lovers of nature, as workers in a profession, so that it may have eternal meaning. Christianity for these men has become an expression of the Ultimate meaning in the action of our daily life. And this is what it should be."[8]

However, in order to fully realize this dynamic identity between the secular and the sacred, the very notion of God must be overcome and be replaced by the notion of sunyata or absolute nothingness. This is not a fight of God against religion within religion, but a fight of sunyata against religion within religion. This is the reason why Zen Buddhism emphasizes:

Encountering a Buddha, killing the Buddha;
Encountering a patriarch, killing the patriarch;
—Only thus does one attain liberation and
disentanglement from all things, thereby becoming
completely unfettered and free.⁹

In the Japanese tradition not only painting and calligraphy but also such mundane activities as drinking tea, arranging flowers, martial arts and so on, have been transformed into ritual, religious practice, under the influence of Zen. They are nonreligious religious practice. The Tea ceremony, for instance, is performed beyond God, or through "killing the Buddha." The Ultimate is fully expressed in such actions of daily life.

Tillich advances the idea of "God above God" in order to demythologize the idea of God and to transcend the theistic notion of God to give a new valuation to secularism. But as I also said in my response to Langdon Gilkey in Boston last December: "If Tillich's phrase 'God above God' still implies yet another 'God' that is above God, as the term is normally understood, then this 'God' cannot really be *above* God at all. If the phrase 'God above God' is truly to signify that which is *above* God or *beyond* God, then what is signified cannot be spoken of as a 'God' at all. In my point of view what is signified must be absolute Nothingness or sunyata."

IV

I referred before to Tillich's notion of dynamic typology which he believed to be the most adequate approach to the history of religions. I share that belief because, unlike Hegel's progressive view of history, Tillich's dynamic typology grasps religions in their particularity and contrasting polarity on the universal religious basis—the experience of the Holy. He also emphasizes that under the method of dynamic typology one religion judges not only other religions but also itself in the light of its encounter with other religions. This is an extremely important issue in understanding the significance of the history of religions for the systematic theologian. In my remaining remarks, I would like to make a critical observation of Tillich in this regard.

To Tillich as a systematic theologian the criterion of judging

NEGATION IN BUDDHISM AND IN TILLICH   95

other religions as well as Christianity itself is the event of the Cross, the image of Jesus as the Christ. I well understand this. As Tillich unambiguously states: "It is natural and unavoidable that Christians affirm the fundamental assertion of Christianity that Jesus is the Christ and reject what denies this assertion."[10]

My question in this connection, however, is how this fundamental Christian assertion can be reconciled with the notion of dynamic typology. Since dynamic typology by definition presupposes the plurality of and interrelationality among various types of religion, it cannot accommodate itself to the Christian assertion of the event of Jesus as the ultimate criterion of judging all religions. And to thoroughly maintain the Christian assertion of the event of Jesus Christ as the ultimate criterion of judging all religions undermines the position of dynamic typology.

Of course, Tillich tries to resolve this issue. On the one hand, he emphasizes that in addition to the interfaith dialogue among various types of religions, the dynamic typological approach includes self-reflection on the part of each religion: "Under the method of dynamic typology every dialogue between religions is accompanied by a silent dialogue *within* the representatives of each of the participating religions."[11] This emphasis is directly linked with another emphasis, that of the importance of self-judgment within Christianity in the light of its encounter with other religions.

On the other hand, Tillich tries to reduce the uniqueness or particularity of the event of Jesus Christ as much as possible to the extent it does not distort the fundamental Christian assertion of Jesus as the Christ: "What is particular in him [Jesus] is that he crucified the particular in himself for the sake of the universal. This liberates his image from bondage both to a particular religion [Judaism] and to the religious sphere as such. . . . With this image, particular yet free from particularity, religious yet free from religion, the criteria are given under which Christianity must judge itself and, by judging itself, judge also the other religions and the quasi-religions."[12]

This is a unique interpretation of the event of the Cross that beautifully reconciles the fundamental assertion of Christianity with the notion of dynamic typology. Speaking from the Buddhist point of view, however, I still see a difficulty in agreeing completely to his interpretation of the event of the Cross as the criterion for judging all religions.

If I am not mistaken, the event of the Cross is the one and only historical event which is, to use Tillich's terminology, the "final

revelation," the last, genuine, decisive, and unsurpassable revelation. And the sole way for us to approach this event is through
participation. This means that "particular yet free from particularity, religious yet free from religion"—the dialectical identity
of particularity and universality, immanence and transcendence,
humanity and divinity—is fully realized *only* in Jesus as the Christ
and other people only *participate* in that dialectical identity, without fully realizing it. This requires that the event of the Cross be
central not only to Christians but to followers of all other religions as well. This is the implication of the idea that the event of
the Cross is the criterion for judging all religions. It also implies
that, as Tillich himself states, "that which has happened there [in
the event of the Cross] in a symbolic way, happens *fragmentarily*
in other places, in other moments, has happened and will happen
even though they are not historically or empirically connected
with the Cross."[13]

This notion of the event of the Cross as the criterion for judging
not only Christianity but also all non-Christian religions is, I am
afraid, not compatible with the dynamic typology of world religions which presupposes the experience of the Holy in everything
finite and particular; nor is it possible for Buddhism to accept such
a position.

V

The basic principle of Buddhism is *pratitya samutpada*, dependent
co-origination. This principle indicates that everything in and out
of the universe is interdependent, co-arising and co-ceasing; nothing exists by itself, independent of other things. This is the reason
Gautama Buddha, the founder of Buddhism, did not accept the
age-old Vedantic notion of Brahman believed to be the ultimate
sole ground of all beings, eternal, unchangeable and substantial.
Instead, he advocated the principle of dependent co-origination,
based on the realization of the impermanence and nonsubstantiality of all things. Under the principle of dependent coorigination, good and evil, being and nothingness, one and many, God and
nature, are *completely* interdependent, co-arising and co-ceasing.
Bonum ipsum, that is, the good itself, Being itself with a capital *B*, the absolute One as the source of the many, and even God
above God are, due to their self-existing nature, regarded from the

Buddhist point of view as unreal, conceptual constructions. The key to the realization of dependent co-origination is to overcome the notion of absolute oneness. Buddhism is neither dualistic nor monistic.

Buddhists have another term for the ultimate reality embodied in the notion of "dependent coorigination": *tathata*, which means "suchness" or "as-it-is-ness." Under the principle of dependent co-origination, everything is realized truly as it is in its suchness or distinctiveness, yet everything is interrelated on the common basis of the realization of the nonsubstantiality or emptiness of all things—even the absolute One is not an exception to this realization.

I believe this Buddhist principle of dependent co-origination provides the best foundation for dynamic typology as an approach to the history of religions. For under the principle of dependent co-origination each and every type of religion is grasped as it is in its suchness or distinctiveness. And yet this does not occur in a confused or chaotic state but in close interrelatedness or typological structure on the common universal basis of emptiness.

In this connection one may then ask, What is the Buddhist criterion of judging itself and other religions? In one sense there is no criterion in Buddhism because Buddhism does not establish any monistic or monotheistic principle such as God, the event of the Cross or Brahman. It tries to overcome *any and all* discrimination in order to attain nondiscrimination, that is, complete equality. Nondiscrimination as the mere negation of discrimination is, however, called in Buddhism false equality, for that would not be true nondiscrimination. Sheer nondiscrimination as the negation of discrimination is still not free from a higher form of discrimination, that is, a discrimination between discrimination and nondiscrimination. True nondiscrimination can be realized only through the negation of nondiscrimination. Here again we need the double negation, the negation of discrimination and the negation of nondiscrimination. Through this double negation, and the realization of sunyata, we arrive at absolute affirmation. That is to say, we come to a clear and definite discrimination through the negation of nondiscrimination. That is the discrimination of nondiscrimination or the discrimination based on nondiscrimination. At that point discrimination as it is, is equality, and equality as it is, is discrimination. The Buddhist criterion for judging itself and all other religions can be found in this dialectical notion of the discrimination of nondiscrimination.

In order to help understand the Buddhist standpoint of the discrimination of nondiscrimination I would like to quote a statement made by a Chinese Zen master, Ch'ing-yan Wei-hsin, who lived in the T'ang dynasty: "Thirty years ago, before I began to study Zen, I said, 'Mountains are mountains; streams are streams.' After I got an insight into the truth of Zen through the instruction of a good master I said, 'Mountains are not mountains; streams are not streams.' But now, having attained the abode of final rest [that is, awakening], I say, 'Mountains are really mountains; streams are really streams.' "[14]

The master's first understanding, "Mountains are mountains; streams are streams," represents a discrimination through objectification. In his second understanding, "Mountains are not mountains; streams are not streams," he overcomes objectification and discrimination and realizes the nondiscrimination of mountains and streams. At this point, however, he is still not completely free of discrimination, for by negating discrimination he remains in nondiscrimination. In order to attain the final state of awakening he must overcome nondiscrimination and thereby attain the third understanding, "Mountains are really mountains; streams are really streams." Here in this final understanding mountains and streams are clearly discriminated in their distinctiveness on the basis of nondiscriminative equality. This is the starting point of Buddhist activity and creativity.

Of course, this dynamic principle of the discrimination of nondiscrimination applies not only to mountains and streams, but to all things, including various world religions. By applying this principle to Christianity and Buddhism in their interfaith dialogue, we might say:

> Before I practised Buddhism I said, "Christianity is Christianity, Buddhism is Buddhism," because I was caught in discrimination.
>
> After I had an insight into the truth of Buddhism I said, "Christianity is not Christianity; Buddhism is not Buddhism" because I broke through the limitation of the particularity of Christianity and Buddhism through the realization of nondiscriminative equality.
>
> But now, by overcoming this nondiscriminative equality in awakening, I say, "Christianity is really Christianity and Buddhism is really Buddhism."

This is a picture of dynamic typology in a Buddhist perspective. If you extend this to other religions you may understand the significance that the history of religions has for the Buddhist systematic theologian.

NOTES

1. Paul Tillich, *The Future of Religions* (New York: Harper and Row, 1966), p. 91 (hereafter cited in text as *FR*).
2. I wrote a review article of this book shortly after its appearance in 1966. The article is included in my book *Zen and Western Thought* (London: Macmillan; Honolulu: Univ. of Hawaii Press, 1986), pp. 171–85.
3. Paul Tillich, *Christianity and the Encounter of the World Religions* (New York: Columbia Univ. Press, 1963), pp. 47–48.
4. Ibid., p. 64.
5. Paul Tillich, *Systematic Theology* (Chicago: Univ. of Chicago Press, 1951), 1:189; idem, *The Courage to Be* (New Haven: Yale Univ. Press, 1957), pp. 34, 40.
6. Tillich, *Christianity and the Encounter*, p. 94.
7. Masao Abe, "Non-Being and *Mu*—the Metaphysical Nature of Negativity in the East and West," in my *Zen and Western Thought*, pp. 121–34.
8. Tillich, *Christianity and the Encounter*, p. 94.
9. *Lin-chi lu*. See Masao Abe, "God, Emptiness, and the True Self," in *Eastern Buddhist* 2, no. 2 (1969): 16.
10. Tillich, *Christianity and the Encounter*, p. 29.
11. Ibid., p. 57.
12. Ibid., pp. 81–82.
13. Ibid., p. 89; italics added.
14. *Wu-teng Hui-yuan* (Japanese *Gotoegen*), ed. Aishin Imaeda (Tokyo: Rinrokaku Shoten, 1971), p. 335. See also Masao Abe, "Zen Is Not a Philosophy, but . . ." in *Zen and Western Thought*, pp. 4–24.

ROBERT P. SCHARLEMANN

8

RESPONSE AND QUERIES

THE SEVERAL essays that make up the preceding chapters not only serve to illuminate different aspects of the questions indicated in our title, *Negation and Theology,* but also provide occasion to press the discussion further by posing some questions. In some cases the questions can be directed to several of the contributors; in other cases, they are related to just one of the essays. In this response, I have formulated questions of both kinds.

Klemm undertakes to show how deconstruction is a kind of negative theology in our time. He interprets Derrida's statement "What I write is not 'negative theology' " to mean that the deconstruction which Derrida practices " 'is like or as' " a negative theology. This interpretation provides the first, "hermeneutical" reading of the relation between deconstruction and negative theology. It is that relation upon which Klemm focuses his discussion; and, instead of understanding the two to include each other, he understands them to be related through a hermeneutical "as"—deconstruction as negative theology, negative theology as deconstruction. Here we might interject a first question. Are the predicates and subjects interchangeable? If deconstruction "is like" negative theology, is theology also "like" deconstruction? Is one of the two the familiar, which can be used to illuminate the unfamiliar? Or can we start with either of the two as the more familiar in order to illuminate the other?

Klemm, in any case, seems to start with the assumption that negative theology is the relatively known, which can be used to interpret deconstruction. Pseudo-Dionysius provides us with a case of negative theology; we can use that negative theology to understand what deconstruction is. What Klemm then regards as "the secret of negative theology," an "open secret" in that negative theology simultaneously reveals and veils what it is about, is "that meditation on the names [of God] leads to God, not by prescribing an agenda for thought or perception, but by opening a way in language"; the "words themselves" open the secret " 'place' " in which meditation can contemplate God. The parallel with what Derrida calls *différance* is clear; *différance* is the "very opening of the space" in which philosophy is produced, and it includes ontotheology but cannot in turn be appropriated by ontotheology. "Opening the space" for the intuition of God beyond being is what Pseudo-Dionysius ascribes to meditation on the divine names; it is what Derrida ascribes to *différance*. Klemm calls this place the "sheer openness of being to thinking and thinking to being." But the critical sentence, which immediately follows, is unclear to me: "The hyperessential God . . . takes place when attention to the openness withdraws and gives way to divine darkness." What kind of occurrence is meant? A two- or three-sentence elaboration of it would help. Does "attention to openness" mean a state of thinking in which one is thinking just about the openness of thinking to being and being to thinking? If so, what does it mean to say that this attention "withdraws" and that "divine darkness" replaces it? Is this to say that I stop thinking and, as I do so, what replaces the openness of thinking to being is a "darkness"? To think of being *as* being is to attend to the openness of being to thinking and thinking to being, it is said; this attention "withdraws," and when it does so—that is, when I am no longer thinking of being as being—what appears is the "darkness" of God. Is that what is meant by that "withdrawing" and "giving way"?

Another question concerns the reference to divine names in Pseudo-Dionysius. Is *God*—the word—itself a name? In Pseudo-Dionysius, the names of God are the titles that can be predicated of God. But this leaves unanswered the question whether *God* itself is a name. In some sense, it must be. But it could be so in the way that a pronoun is a name or in the way that a proper name is a name or in the way that a common noun is a name. In any of those three cases, one would still need to take account of the difference between the name that points out, or shows, what one is even talking about and the name or names that can be predicated of the one shown. If *God* is not a name, what is it? If it is a name, what is the difference between its functioning and the functioning of the predicative names?

Klemm proceeds to ask whether Derrida's *différance* might be a divine name. If it is such, then, like the other divine names, it "opens the place" of the dwelling of God, although it is not an appropriation of God. *Différance,* Derrida says, cannot be reappropriated ontologically or theologically—that is, philosophically, since "philosophy" for Derrida means ontotheology—because *différance* opens the space in which philosophy works. Is this lack of appropriability what Klemm refers to as the divine darkness? Klemm asks, "Is '*différance*' somehow a divine name?" Should the question perhaps read: "Is the practice of meditating on the divine names analogous to the writing of *différance*?" This formulation of the question would suggest that the writing of *différance* and the meditation on the divine names are ways in which the writer (reader) and the meditator clear the "space" within which both being and God appear without being capable of appropriation by the writer or the meditator. That Derrida does not consider deconstruction to be negative theology, Klemm grants; and he suggests that reading it as a version of such cannot be carried through— for doing so would amount to an "annexing" of it by a "good will to power." A parallel problem appears in a purely deconstructive reading. This is what leads to Klemm's suggestion that deconstruction cannot be absorbed by hermeneutics nor hermeneutics by deconstruction. The two are an irreducible polarity. Here, I think, is the point of difference between Klemm and Taylor. Taylor sets unity and difference against each other, and argues against unity for difference. Klemm argues for the irreducibility of the hermeneutical and the deconstructive, and this seems to amount to the irreducibility of identity to difference or difference to identity.

Because the hermeneutical reading ends at a point where the good will of the reader is shown to be a "will to power" over the text (and the will to power that the text discloses in the reader interpreting it is thus exhibited by the text itself), Klemm tries a second reading, which takes this outcome as a clue: the rhetorical reading tries to uncover a will to power in deconstruction. According to this rhetorical reading, the statement that deconstruction "is not" negative theology means that deconstruction "is a sign of something other" than negative theology. I take this formulation to mean that deconstruction neither is nor is not negative theology, so that trying to determine whether deconstruction is negative theology is like trying to determine, let us say, whether a rock is or is not happiness. The concepts of happiness and rock can not be predicated of each other, but it is possible that saying, or writing, that a rock is not happiness might itself signify the "otherness" that is between the subject term and predicate term of the proposition. (Rocks and happiness do not belong to the same language game, Wittgenstein might say. The only game in which a statement like "A rock is happiness" might occur is a game that tries to show the difference between the language game in which one speaks of empirical objects, like rocks, and the language game in which one speaks of happiness. Saying "A rock is happiness" might thus be a way of pointing to a language game other than the one in which empirically perceptible and abstractly conceivable predications can be made of rocks.) In this sense, the statement "Deconstruction is not negative theology" would serve to signify the otherness between the two that makes them incomparable. If this is the case, however, then it would not be true, as Klemm writes, that deconstruction "supersedes ontotheology," and the implication that Klemm sees in the quotation from Derrida would not really be in Derrida's statement. What is not clear to me, in Klemm's explanation, is whether he is saying that deconstruction is not negative theology, but is a replacement for the old ontotheology, which related being and God in the midst (the "space") of the difference between them, or that deconstruction is not negative theology because it is something else altogether. The latter, which makes more of the reinforced (or even doubled) negation connoted by the *de* of *dénégations,* seems to be the intention in the remaining portion of this part of his essay. My question is simply whether I have read that intention correctly or perhaps missed it entirely.

Since the result of this part of the analysis is to show that the "good will to power" is itself a variation on the hermeneutical reading, with the consequence that the rhetorical and the hermeneutical cannot be disengaged from each other, the "good will to power" both is and is not understood. Hermeneutics and deconstruction, therefore, both undergo a reversal in the confrontation. Klemm asks whether the clash between them helps bring out a new negative theology, and he suggests that an affirmative answer to the question lies in a negative theology in which God is named as "the overturning"—God is God as the overturning of the one by the other. This, obviously, is a theme that cannot be developed in the course of his essay. Hence, the only question I might ask about it is similar to my other questions. To say that God "is God as" something seems to be different from predicating names of God. The "God is Goodness," as in the treatises on the divine names, is of another type than would be "God is God as Goodness." Is the "is . . . as" intended to be a kind of predication which formulates the "neither is nor is not" of traditional negative theology? Or does it have some other purpose?

Mark Taylor's essay evokes somewhat different but still related questions. Like Derrida, Taylor's style exhibits a certain practice that makes it different from the expository writing one learned in college. An example appears in the first paragraph in what follows the sentence "Nothing is, after all, always the question." It is the "after all" in the sentence (which one tends to pass over quickly while reading) that provokes the next thoughts, involving the difference between the "after-all" and the "before-all" and the relations of repetition and reflection. Such stylistic features are part of the "errancy" of Taylor's writing, as of Derrida's, and they should be taken as essential to the whole meaning. But for present purposes, I want to put them aside in order to pose some questions about the conceptual content of the essay.

How many ways of thinking naught are there? Taylor indicates at least two: (1) not thinking at all, and (2) thinking, but thinking of the negative meant by "naught," or thinking nothing. Initially, it might occur to us that not thinking and thinking nothing amount to the same. If one is thinking nothing, one must not be thinking; and if one is not thinking, one must be thinking nothing. But Taylor makes the sound point that there is more than a linguistic difference between "not thinking anything" and "thinking nothing." Not to think anything indicates the absence of the activity of thinking; to think nothing, or naught, indicates that there is an activity of thinking going on but the "object" of which one is thinking is nothing. This is a thinking activity that cannot be completed because its object is always missing; and this naught is in turn neither being nor nonbeing—it neither is nor is not anything one might think of as an object. In the rest of the essay, then, Taylor undertakes to suggest an alternative, still "untried," to a conservative, a liberal, or a dialectical understanding of God, when "dialectical" refers to a theological thinking in which the negative serves only as a transition to a deeper positive, "a higher positivity." The untried path is to think the thought "Nothing is divine" (rather than "God is nothing") or to think the incompleteness of the order of representation from which one cannot escape, a "non-negative negative a/theology." Why not, rather, a double starting point—"Nothing is God" and "God is nothing"? (And is it not important to say "Nothing is God" rather than "Nothing is divine"?)

The path so indicated is not meant to suggest that such phrasings as "neither being nor nonbeing" have never occurred in theology. Even the medieval tale of the monk who described the beyond as *nec aliter nec taliter sed totaliter aliter*—neither the same nor different but totally different—formulates it. More recently, Tillich's essay on the idea of a theology of culture contains a similar wording. One would be surprised, however, to discover the phrase "non-negative negative a/theology" prior to Taylor—a nicely tailored phrasing, if one might put it so, because the *negative* that follows the *non-negative* forestalls making out of the negation of negation a positive and the *a/theology* suggests a theology that is not implicated in the alternative of the negative of atheism and the positive of theism. But three questions arise. First, is the problem of thinking "naught," to which the essay is devoted, specifically the problem of thinking naught as the *subject* of a predication (as in "Nothing is divine")? Second, what is the difference between saying "Nothing is divine" and "Nothing is God"? Finally, what would one need to find in the writings of an author, say, those of Pseudo-Dionysius, in order for him to be, or to be understood as, one who thought the "naught"?

Another kind of question concerns the meaning of identity and difference. In Taylor's essay, a reader could easily confuse "the one" of mystical theology with "identity," as though speaking of God as "the one" beyond being and nonbeing were equivalent to speaking of God as identity beyond difference. Is it the intention to equate unity (the one) and identity in this way? It would seem to me that the "one" of mystical theology is not identity, as opposed to difference, but a category other than identity and difference; and the distinction seems important.

Edith Wyschogrod's essay provides occasion to go even further into the question of negation. Her essay is a thesis about Derrida to the effect that his no-saying is best expressed by the French particle *nulle part*, "nowhere without no." Wyschogrod calls attention to the fact that, in English, there is sometimes a difference between saying "not a" or "not any" and "no," whereas at other times there is no such difference. "There are not any cookies in the jar" and "There are no cookies in the jar" say the same; but "He is not an English gentleman" and "He is *no* English gentleman" say something different, as would "This is not a cookie" and "This is no cookie," to cite another kind of illustration. Such differences, however, do not correspond to different ways of negating in French, where negatives are often composite. (Is it true, though, that the *de* in "Il ne cesse de gronder" really forms part of the negative? Is it not rather that a *pas* is dropped or presupposed, and that the *de* has the sense of "from"—"He does not stop [from] grumbling"?) Now, Derrida is stationed, in Wyschogrod's analysis, between two positions, the one of which holds that we are the origin of the *not* and the other that the *not* is the origin of our saying "not" or "no." These are the two positions between which Heidegger seeks an adjudication in "What Is Metaphysics?" where he concludes that, contrary to positivism, the *not* is the origin of our thinking the negative. Wyschogrod sees in Derrida's position something that is between those two possibilities, so that the task is not to decide for the one or the other of the two sides of the alternative but to see what is between them. How does one describe such a position between the two? Wyschogrod does so by using Bergson, especially in Deleuze's reading of him, and Levinas as representing the two opposites, Bergson's nonbeing as subjective and Levinas's otherness as a hypostatization; and for purposes of classifying the positions, she uses the several ways of expressing negation in French. Derrida is tied to Bergson by way of the *jamais* and to Levinas by way of *nul(le)*, with Derrida's own position located between them and indicated by *nulle part*, "nowhere" or "nowhere without no."

Part of the problem with which both Derrida and Levinas struggle is that of engaging in thinking without doing so ontologically. But Derrida, as Wyschogrod's analysis goes on to show, develops Levinas's thought at two levels. One is that of thinking the Good, which is not "ontological" and "categorial" because it is "projected toward the other"; this is at the edge of philosophy (ontology) but still within it. The second is that of an ethics "governed by the rule of desire." A thinking that is governed by desire is no longer metaphysical, or ontotheological, because it can never find fulfillment in objects of its satisfaction. Such desire can be expressed in language by the vocative case. But Levinas differs from "traditional negative theology" because an infinite distance is maintained between the interlocutor and addressee; the one addressed is absolutely exterior to the thinker, and there is, therefore, no unity of "theoretical objectivity" and "mystical communion." This "one" is absolutely exterior but "unknowable and thus a 'not anyone.'" Wyschogrod summarizes her analysis by noting that this view of the Other "is governed by the negative particle *nul / nulle*" not in the sense of anyone-but-no-one-in-particular but rather in the sense of the Other of anyone and everyone. It is this *nul(le)* who appeals and commands. In other words, the negative theology associated with mysticism is a form of negation that passes beyond all things to a union with God as the one beyond being; Levinas's path leads beyond all things, beyond being, not to union with the one but to absolute distance from the Other who calls and commands. What Derrida and Levinas are, therefore, putting into contrast are (1) the "traditional" negative theology, whose attitude is that of theoretical objectivity—contemplation, let us say—and whose aim is absorption into the one, and (2) a Levinasian negative theology in which the attitude is not theoretical (contemplation) but ethical (call and hearkening) and in which the end is not absorption of the thinker into the one beyond being but radical distance between the Other who commands and the thinker who hearkens. Could one say—this is a question to Wyschogrod—that Levinas represents a combination of the negation characteristic of mystical theology with the encounter characteristic of Buber's "Thou"? Would such a reference to Buber be misleading in a description of Levinas's Derrida?

Another question arises in connection with the next point. Still in the context of Derrida's analysis of Levinas, Wyschogrod speaks of the problem that arises when "metaphysics is *identified* with speech" (emphasis hers). What is the sense or meaning of such an identification? What would I be doing if I identified metaphysics and speech? What is it that is being identified with speech, and in what way is the "identification" expressed? Presumably not in the statement "Metaphysics is speech," which is not likely to appear anywhere either in a work on metaphysics or in a metaphysical work. Is "the discourse of metaphysics" the discourse which says that something is something (e.g., "Speech is the defeat of violence")?

Wyschogrod's conclusion is, in any case, that Derrida's deconstructive negation differs from a negation designed to stress divine perfections. "God is unlimited" would be a statement in traditional mystical or negative theology; divine perfection is expressed as the negation of all limitation. What would be a deconstructive counterpart of such a statement? Would it be a statement on the order of "God is neither limited nor unlimited" (the sense of which would be to refer us beyond the category of limitation altogether)? In that case, Tillich's statement that God is the "ground of being," in which "ground of being" is a metaphor, or "symbolic concept," as Tillich calls it (*Systematic Theology*, 1:156), might be a deconstructive version of negative theology. Or *can* a deconstructive negative theological statement even be made?

The second difference between Derrida and negative theology of divine perfection which Wyschogrod notes is that Derrida "privileges a . . . temporalization that cannot be made present," the no-saying of *ja-mais*, of the always-already-no-longer. This would be in part similar (if I may extrapolate) to what appears in the Augustinian meditation on the temporal "now," which is always already past when we name or grasp it, but in part different from the Augustinian in that it does not look toward an "eternal now," a *nunc stans*, but toward something else. "Toward what else?" might be the question to pose here. Perhaps toward an unending flow? Or toward what is quite other than time and temporality and therefore not conceivable either as an eternal now or as an unending restlessness?

The third contrast Wyschogrod makes is between Derrida's explication of the Other who is "excluded from language" (but speaks and hears) and classical negative theology whose object is beyond language but is somehow "linked up" with language, or with "the speech of historical time and prayer of invocation." Is this, in less exact but perhaps more indicative terms, the difference between saying, on one side, "God speaks and hears, but there are no words that are God's words (divine words instead of human words) and no particular entity to whom we can speak as to God" and saying, on the other side, "God is beyond language, but there are some words that are God's words, not merely human words, and there are some entities to whom we can speak as to God"? In this latter case, prophetic words (for example) might be unlike other words in being the message of God, even if the message of God as such is "beyond" those words; in the former case, prophetic words would be human words on a par with all other human words, even when the Other speaks through them.

Such a difference between "deconstructive" and "hyperessential" negative theology can be made independently of the historical question whether the thinkers found in the catalogue of mystical or negative theologians do fit the description of "hyperessential" negation rather than "deconstructive negation." But if this is a description of the difference between the two, then we have a way of seeing the place at which Wyschogrod is locating Levinas's negative theology.

Finally, a question arises between Klemm's and Wyschogrod's

chapters. In Klemm's account, *différance* seems, in Derrida, to name the "place" *within which* being and nonbeing can appear; in Wyschogrod's account, *chōra* seems to name the "place" within which even *différance* appears. Is my reading of Klemm's and Wyschogrod's interpretations here correct?

In her essay, Jane Mary Trau is concerned with the formulation of the trinitarian doctrine, a theological dogma peculiar to the Christian understanding of deity and one whose course toward acceptance was a rocky one. The efforts to formulate the dogma of a three-in-one deity can be seen against the divided background of early Christian theology. Part of the background is provided by New Testament assertions about Jesus, the Father of Jesus, and the Spirit sent by Jesus or by Jesus and the Father. Another part of it is provided by a philosophical conception according to which anything that is real is so by its constitution as an individual of a species of a genus. The relation of the three in the one reality is that the individual is the accidental appearance, the species is the essential form, and the genus is the ground of the form. Thus, on the one hand the threefoldness of deity originates in the biblical language; on the other hand, it originates in a conception of what belongs to the fullness of the real. Uniting these two, diverse parts of the background was a major motif in the trinitarian formulations. In being real, deity had a threefoldness, like any real entity. Like a genus, which served as the ground of the specific differences, the Father was the basis of the deity, the *fons et origo* or generating power; like a species, the Son was the essential form of deity, the *Logos* of God; and like an individual, the Spirit was the occasional (and rationally underivable) way in which deity appeared in different places. That much of the doctrine reflected the relations of genus, species, and individual in any reality. But a strict parallel between the two series of terms was prevented both by the notion that each of the three personae of the one God is in a sense the one and only God and also by the confluence of the trinitarian and the christological discussions, according to which, if taken at face value, the second persona of the deity had two natures, the divine and the human, incompatible with each other. Although monotheism does not of itself require that the one and only God can only be one, that is, completely identical with itself in its deity, monotheistic thought has always meant both that there is only one God and that God is only one, that is, identical with God as God. The trinitarian element is the concept that this one and only God, eternally identical in its deity, is also eternally differentiated without a disruption of its unity and identity. To state it so is simultaneously to indicate the formidable conceptual problems a tri-unitarian idea of monotheistic deity entails. That Trau undertakes a proposal concerning this problem is itself noteworthy, but that it is done with a view to a revised modalist conception makes it doubly interesting.

Where does the problem lie? The Son is not the Father, the Father is not the Son, and yet each of them is wholly God and the only God. How is it conceivable that the one is *not* the other if the basis for distinguishing between them, or the basis on which it is possible for the one *not* to be the other, seems to be absent? This is the question. We have no problem with thinking of the difference between a maple and an oak (if maple and oak are taken to be species of a genus); a maple is not an oak, but each of the two is generically a tree. But we would have a problem thinking of the difference between them if it were said that a maple is not an oak, and an oak not a maple, but that both the maple and the oak are the one and only tree there is. The problem with the trinitarian doctrine is that, on the one hand, the doctrine explicates the sense in saying that God is real, a unity of individual in a species of a genus, but, on the other hand, the doctrine denies that the paternity of God is related to the Son and Spirit in the manner of the genus of deity to the form and accidence of the appearance of deity. Half of the parallel makes sense. It is as the Son that deity appears in form; it is as the Spirit that deity is individualized in its proper appearance; it is as the Father that deity is the principle or origin of the appearance and the individual properties. The other half of the parallel breaks down. For, unlike a species, the Son is not only the form of appearance of the Father but is the fullness of deity coequal and coeternal with the Father; and, unlike the individual, the Spirit not only is the individualizing property of the Son and Father but is coequal and coeternal with them. Moreover, unlike a genus, which can be predicated of the species as well as of the individual, fatherhood cannot be predicated of the Son and the Spirit; there is a fourth element (deity; God) besides the three that constitute a parallel with the genus, species, and individual. Hence, the trinitarian debates oscillated between a kind of quatri-unity, with deity itself as a fourth principle besides the Father, Son, and Spirit, and a kind of binitarianism, with fatherhood as equivalent to deity itself, with sonship as the form of appearance, and with spirit as the individualizing properties. Finally, unlike the elements of genus, species, and individual, each of the three

personae is an individual. This description puts into other words
the problem Trau takes up in terms of the "identity of indiscernibles" but also presents other aspects in the background of the
trinitarian problem.

The problem in this dogma is to explain "how Jesus, the Son"
can be "numerically distinct yet substantially identical" with the
Father. "How can we reconcile" there being "only one God" with
"three individuals" who are God but "not three Gods"? This is
Trau's question. We might think of the problem in this way. Two
maple trees are numerically distinct and they *are essentially* identical (they are both maple trees), but they *are not substantially*
identical because the individualization of the essence in the one
is different from its individualization in the other maple tree. The
Son and the Father of the Trinity are numerically distinct and *are
essentially* identical (they are both divine, or deity), but they *are
also substantially* identical because their individualizing of deity
is the same in both cases. But, if this is so of the Son and the Father,
then it is problematic how the two can be distinct individuals,
for "the discernibility of individuals relies on their having distinct
properties and substance." That is to say, we could not tell the difference between two individual maple trees if there were not an
individual substance (*ousia*) for the generic nature (the *physis*) and
if this individual substance were not the bearer of the properties of
the individual. If there were no such substance and properties, we
would not say about a second maple tree, "This is another maple,"
but we would say, instead, "This is the maple again." In other
words, there must be not only specific properties, which make it
possible to distinguish between a maple tree and an oak tree, but
also individual properties, which make it possible to distinguish
between one maple tree and another maple tree. Now, if there is
one and only one God, how can the Father (who is not the Son)
and the Son (who is not the Father) be the one and only God? This
is not the problem of explaining that a maple, an oak, and an elm
can all be trees since they are different trees and the nature (or
physis) of a tree is what "generates" both the identity and the difference. It is, rather, like the problem of conceiving how a maple,
an oak, and an elm, though different from each other, could each
be the one and only tree. There would be no problem with explaining how three maple trees can all be maples, since they are three
individual substances (*ousiai*) of the form (or species) of maple.
But there would be a problem if we tried to conceive how each
of three individual maple trees, though different from each other,

is the one and only species maple. These perplexities are com-
pounded in the trinitarian formulations by their convergence with
the christological formulations. For the Son in the Trinity is one of
the three personae of the divine nature, or *physis*, but also has two
physeis, a human and a divine; and human is what God as God is
not and God is what man as man is *not*. Thus, there is a unity of
being and not being divine (or of being divine and not divine) in
the second persona of the Godhead, which nonetheless, does not
diminish the divinity of God's being.

Modalism in the early church offered a solution: the "persons"
of the Trinity are ways in which God is God, or modes of God's
being. God is God as Father (begetter, generator; like a genus); God
is God as Son (begotten, logos; like a species); God is God as Spirit
(unity of begetter and begotten; like the individual unity of genus
and species). But, in that case, the personae cannot be thought of as
individual substances, for only the Father is "first *ousia*" or "persona." Trau, therefore, proposes a variation on modalism, which is
designed to conceive what early modalism did not conceive: that
there are three ways of God's existing and that these three ways
are also three individual substances.

What this means we might seek to indicate initially by a parallel with the examples we have just used. A maple, an oak, and an
elm would have to be conceived not just as three ways in which
a tree is a tree but also as three individual substances of the tree.
The prime substance, or first *ousia*, as Trau is using the concept,
is the common substance of accidents; the secondary substance,
or second *ousia*, is the common substratum of the individual substances. Let us say that, in our example, "maple" designates the
first *ousia* (contained in the concept of a maple as a maple tree)
of the accidents (the shape of the leaves, the bark, and whatever
other features make an actual tree recognizable as a maple), and
that the second *ousia* designates the features that would be found
in any individual maple (not belonging to the concept of maple
but nonetheless always found present in maples). Persona comes
into the picture as the Latin equivalent of first *ousia*, while adding
to it some legal connotations of property.

Trau takes as the starting point for her revision of this modalism
the oneness of God but adds to it that every reality is symbolic:
"The divine nature [is] manifested by one and only one being,
which is by nature symbolic." There is, in other words, a divine
"nature" of God, according to which there can be only one God.

But this nature is symbolic, a nature that maintains itself as it expresses or transcends itself in its other; the pluralities in which it expresses itself reveal it without fragmenting or diffusing the self that is the nature. Thus, if the nature "tree" is symbolized in a maple, an oak, and an elm, then the individual maple is no less "the tree" than is the oak or the elm. A symbol in that sense represents, it makes present again, the one and only nature which it symbolizes; and in that sense, it is an "extension of the unity" even though it is not numerically identical to that primordial unity. As a result, the symbol is, paradoxically when compared with other entities, an individual without being a "first *ousia*." There is another paradox in the trinitarian conception in the fact that the first *ousia* (the divine nature) is also the second *ousia* (the common properties of the individuals); the nature that is symbolized is also the symbol that symbolizes it. The Trinity is understood, then, as three symbolic expressions of the second *ousia* (that is, of the common properties of God in all the appearances of God) but not of the first *ousia* (or the substance in the concept of God as God). To the objection that, if Father, Son, and Spirit are symbols and not persons, they cannot be themselves divine, Trau responds with the reminder that a symbol makes present the *ousia* that it expresses. But is each of the symbols then "fully divine"? Trau replies that each is fully divine but none exhausts the divine nature. Each of them is, we might say, the one and only God, but none of them exhausts the ways in which God can be God.

In sum, we can say that the concept of symbol, as Trau employs it, makes it possible to explain how three different expressions of God can be fully God (the one and only God), or how God can be God in three different ways so that each of the three ways is an individualized expression of the fullness of the deity as deity. The "ontology of the symbol" is difficult to grasp, as Trau puts it, because it is paradoxical: a symbol "is what it is not." This remark can serve as the occasion for putting a question about the proposal she is making. I shall leave aside some questions about the trinitarian formulations themselves (such as the relation of *ousia* and *hypostasis* or of *hypostasis, prosōpon* and persona or of *physis* and *ousia*) in order to concentrate on the main question here. The question is derived from there seeming to be nothing in the notion of symbol, just as there is nothing in the notion of person, to account for the three of the Trinity. If that is the case, what is the root or rationale of the threeness of divine being? Why just three symbols of the one God? Might the answer to this question not lie in the being and not being implied in saying that a symbol "is what it is not"? Are there three symbols because the being of God is a unity of being and not being God in God? It seems to me that we have two choices in formulating a trinitarian doctrine. One is to derive the threeness from the unity of genus, species, and individual in anything real; the other is to derive the threeness from the identity and difference of being and not being. In the former case, the genus is the ground of the same and the different in the species, and the individual is the occasional (unpredictable and unknowable) location at which the species may appear. Then the language of Father, Son, and Spirit can be taken to be a formulation of the way in which deity is real: the Son and the Spirit proceed from the Father, the Logos is the form of deity (like a species, except that there is only one), and the Spirit is the occasional location (the where and when) at which the Logos of deity may appear (like an individual, except that there is only one). In the second case— when the threeness of deity is related to the identity and difference of being and not being—the Father is God's being as God, the Son is God's being as not God (or God's not being God), and the Spirit is the living mediation of being and not being God in the one who is named deity. Trau's revised modalism seems to mix the two patterns indicated by these choices. That is the reason for my posing the question as I have done.

Langdon Gilkey's and Masao Abe's essays both provide comparisons of Buddhist concepts of nothingness and Tillich's concept of God or being. The questions which arise from them can, therefore, be formulated in view of both of them. And since they are thoroughgoing questions, they will implicitly be related to the other essays as well.

Starting with the recognition that, in Tillich's thought, nonbeing is not a simple opposite of God but is "an essential ingredient" in the divine activity, Gilkey undertakes an exploration of the relation between this concept of the negative and the negative in Mahayana Buddhism; he does so by reference to Nishitani Keiji and Tanabe Hajime, both of whom, despite their differences, represent "a common stance" over against Tillich. The aim is to present the "remarkable similarities" and "one or two significant differences" in each case. The similarities between Tillich and Nishitani, both of whom were influenced by classical German philosophy as well as by Nietzsche and Heidegger and both of whom are like Tillich in being primarily theologians as well, are connected with the way in which each of them interprets the religious tradition in relation to the modern understanding of experience. Thus, nihility in Nishitani is not "an objective ontological structure" but an expression of "the absolute threat of destructive nonbeing," for Nishitani, just as the symbols and analysis of negation and the negative in Tillich are expressions of an experience of nonbeing and not references to an objective structure accessible without experience. Again, Tanabe's metanoesis arose out of the experience of collapse in the imperial Japan of 1943–45, just as Tillich's theology was formed by his experience of collapse in World War I and Religious Socialism. The difference between Nishitani and Tillich concerns the question whether the Christian conception of the *will* of God is only a "projection (onto nothingness) of human self-will," that is, a nondialectical category (and hence to be negated, as in Nishitani, when nihility shows the emptiness of everything, or whether it is a dialectical category (and hence to be affirmed in the "courage to be a self" despite the shock of nonbeing. Nishitani dissolves the self and world in nothingness; Tillich reaffirms them in a restoration beyond the nothingness. The "no-self" of Nishitani and the "restored self" of Tillich represent sharply different views of the relation to culture and history.

Gilkey formulates the difference between Tanabe and Tillich by reference to the question of theonomy. Tanabe's argument is that "theonomy is possible only if the Other Power be nothingness"; Tillich's argument is that God as being-itself dialectically affirms and denies "the absoluteness and the immanence of God," so that God is neither "an absolute that swallows up . . . the autonomy of creatures" nor an absolute set heteronomously over against them. Tillich's "theonomous concept of being" therefore requires relating being dialectically to nonbeing so that "God is enabled . . . to function both as being and as nothingness." In short, for Buddhism, as represented in these two thinkers, nothingness depends as much on the finite as the finite on nothingness; nothingness "flows into and through the relative." For Tillich, God, who is both "the source and fulfillment of creation" as well as "a negation of its estranged actuality," must represent "neither absolute being nor absolute nothingness" but "a dialectical polarity of being and nonbeing."

Abe shares with Gilkey the conclusion that Tillich's and Buddhism's concepts of the negative are in the end different from each other. But Abe adds to this a criticism of Tillich's view; he therefore takes us, like Gilkey, beyond a simple analysis of the two concepts to the question of fundamental views of reality, but he does so from the standpoint of one who affirms the Buddhist rather than Tillich's Christian conception of being and nonbeing. Moreover, his analysis itself reveals some aspects of the concept of the negative that do not come into play in Gilkey's analysis. Abe sees "a parallel of sorts" between Tillich's approach to the history of religions, which Tillich called a "free" approach in contrast to the "orthodox-exclusive" and the "secular-rejective" ones, and the approach taken by Mahayana Buddhism in its criticism of Theravada Buddhism. Mahayana Buddhism can be seen to reject the "orthodox-exclusive" and the "secular-rejective" attitudes to a history of religions that Tillich also rejects. Abe then goes on to describe Tillich's approach in more detail and its envisagement of the telos of the history of religions in a "religion of the concrete spirit." To this he adds Tillich's application of the Protestant principle, which, according to Abe, is "strikingly similar to the principle of Mahayana Buddhism" when Mahayana Buddhism asserts that "one should not abide in nirvana in order to fulfil compassion." In nirvana one is not yet entirely free of attachment and selfishness because "in enjoying one's own wisdom and salvation, one may forget the suffering of one's fellow human beings still involved in the flux of samsara." Freedom from attachment both to nirvana and to samsara is, instead, the realization of sunyata, which is "not a nihilistic emptiness" but a "dynamic fullness." Sunyata can be realized "only through the double negation of samsara and nirvana" and this implies that one must move between the two without becoming attached to either. "This dynamic free movement between samsara and nirvana, between the secular and the sacred, is nirvana in the true Mahayanic sense." This is to say that the ultimate in Mahayana Buddhism is sunyata as a "dynamic fullness" that is "both samsara and nirvana and neither samsara nor nirvana at one and the same time." After setting forth those apparent similarities between Tillich's Protestant principle and Mahayana Buddhism, Abe continues by asking whether the two principles, the Protestant and the Mahayanic, are as similar as they appear to be. To this question he gives a negative answer for the reason that sunyata, unlike the Protestant principle, involves a double negation of the secular and sacred which is simultaneously a double affirmation. "Negation of negation is nothing but affirmation of affirmation; absolute negation itself absolute affirmation." The intention of this is made clearer by the statement that "the

secular as it is, is sacred" and "the sacred as it is, is the secular."
In short, the double negation is a dynamic identity.

Abe sees this as different from Tillich's Protestant conception of
God because being and nonbeing in their polarity do not, in Tillich,
"represent a symmetrical correlation." For corroboration he quotes
Tillich's statement that "being precedes nonbeing in ontological
validity, as the word nonbeing itself indicates." One might note,
parenthetically, that the last part of Tillich's sentence would not
be true if, like Hegel, he were using the terms *Sein* and *Nichts*
or *being* and *not* to name the polarity. That Tillich seems to have
equated the polarity of *Sein* and *Nichts* with that of *being* and *nonbeing* may reinforce Abe's point. Hence, Abe can argue that sunyata, as the ultimate, is a fuller and more thorough realization of
the dynamic identity of the secular and sacred ("sunyata is neither
being nor nothingness and yet both being and nothingness") and
that the history of religions is not a struggle of God against religion within religion, as Tillich contended, but a struggle of sunyata against religion within religion. He contends further that the
"very notion of God" must be overcome for the full realization of
the dynamic identity of the sacred and secular. When one takes
into account his interpretation of the symbol of the cross as well,
then his conception comes closer to that of sunyata; but Abe argues, even so, that making this symbol the criterion not only of
Christianity but of all religions is in conflict with the dynamic
typology of world religions and incompatible with Buddhism's,
the principle of dependent coorigination, which Abe considers to
provide "the best foundation" for a dynamic typology of the history of religions. He concludes his description with a nice statement of the progression from the recognition that "Christianity
is Christianity, Buddhism is Buddhism" to the recognition that
"Christianity is not Christianity, Buddhism is not Buddhism" to
the recognition, finally, that "Christianity is really Christianity
and Buddhism is really Buddhism."

Gilkey's and Abe's discussions of Tillich's theology offer the
occasion, now, to formulate some of the most basic questions concerned in negation and theology. The first of them involves the
concept of being-itself. Gilkey points out that, in Tillich, the concept of being-itself does not exclude but includes nonbeing; God
conceived as being-itself is not the exclusion of nonbeing but the
dialectical relation of being and nonbeing. This account seems to
concur with Abe in ascribing to being (in Tillich's thought) a pri-

ority over nonbeing. So we might put the question to Gilkey. Does
Gilkey understand Tillich to be saying that the concept of being-
itself, while including nonbeing, subordinates nonbeing to being?
Or are being and nonbeing on a par ("a symmetrical correlation,"
in Abe's phrase), with no subordination of the one to the other?
Abe wants to maintain, against Tillich's position, that being and
nonbeing (or being and nothing) are on a par so that the two are
never fused in a third, not even the third of being-itself, but there
is a dynamic movement between them in sunyata. This question
to Gilkey, in other words, concerns the interpretation of Tillich.
Does Tillich conceive of being-itself as a third in which being
and nonbeing are united? Does he subordinate nonbeing to being?
Are being and nonbeing united in such a way that being is given
priority over nonbeing, as the very terminology suggests?

We can put a different question to Abe. It is, he argues, sunyata,
and not God, which is the ultimate because sunyata is "neither
being nor nothingness" and yet "both being and nothingness,"
whereas God is being-itself rather than nothing. There seems to be
a clear difference in the predications being made. God "is" being
itself and "is not" nothing; sunyata "is" and "is not" being and "is"
and "is not" nothingness. On the one side, then, "is and is not"
both "being and nothing" and, on the other side, "is" being but "is
not" nothing describe the difference between sunyata and God. For
this reason, Abe thinks that the very notion of God has to be given
up. But here we can put a question to Abe. Although it might be
argued that the polarity of being and nonbeing in Tillich's ontological structure is not meant to be the same as the polarity of
being and nothing (hence Tillich's comments on being and nonbeing would not be applicable to the question of being and nothingness), let us assume for present purposes that they are the same
and that, therefore, Abe is correct in interpreting Tillich to give an
absolute priority to being over nothing. What would Abe say—this
is my question—if another theologian were to understand "God"
to mean one who "is neither being nor nothingness and yet both
being and nothingness"? Would the names "God" and "sunyata"
then be equivalent in meaning? And would it then make any difference whether one said the history of religions is a struggle "of
God against religion within religion" (as Tillich does) or a struggle
"of sunyata against religion within religion" (in Abe's adaptation)?
In such a case, would there be any way of deciding between "God"
and "sunyata"? Or is there something in the meaning of "God"
that would prevent one from so understanding God?

Finally, I should like to turn the question to Gilkey, not as a question about Tillich's theology but as a question about Gilkey's. Would Gilkey say that "being" and "nothing" (the "not" of "nonbeing") are a "symmetrical" polarity (like such polarities as freedom and destiny, dynamics and form) or would he say that the polarity is asymmetrical because nonbeing is derivative from being, but not conversely, and nonbeing is conquered by being, but not conversely?

NOTE

Because of his retirement and move from the University of Chicago, Professor Gilkey was unable to find the time to reply to these queries. He entrusts their answers to the readers.—Ed.

DAVID KLEMM

9

REPLIES

PROFESSOR SCHARLEMANN places four questions (or groups of questions) directly to my essay, to which I will respond in turn. He begins by characterizing my essay as an attempt "to show how deconstruction is a kind of negative theology in our time." From this observation, Scharlemann asks his first question about the logical form of such a judgment. Are the subjects and predicates interchangeable? Is one the more familiar which can be used to illuminate the unfamiliar? According to Scharlemann, my essay proceeds under the assumption that Pseudo-Dionysius provides a paradigm instance of "negative theology." I assume that if one is clear about its concept, then one can use some of its elements to interpret the less well known "deconstruction." Scharlemann raises the possibility that one could equally well speak of negative theology as a kind of deconstruction. In this latter case, one would begin by defining deconstruction and then on that basis describe negative theology. Does not my procedure reflect only one of two possibilities? Let me respond by clarifying my aim.

I take up the question of the relationship between negative theology and deconstruction partly in direct response to the power of Derrida's strategies of writing (which are reminiscent of the *via negativa*) and partly because Derrida himself poses the question and evades its direct answer. In "Comment ne pas parler: dénégations," a key essay for anyone interested in the possible theological significance of deconstruction, Derrida seems both to affirm and to reject the suggestion of resemblance between negative theology and deconstruction. What does this mean for understanding Derrida and deconstruction? I pursue this question by interpreting Derrida's statement "What I write is not 'negative theology.'"

In doing so, I explore Derrida's observation that negative theology and deconstruction share certain features. I follow Derrida's own analysis when I focus on Pseudo-Dionysius as exemplar of negative theology, by means of whose concept one could try to understand deconstruction. I do not reflect on the logical relation of the subject and predicate terms for the purpose of such a comparison, nor do I reflect on the different senses of "being" appropriate to the relatively particular referent of the subject term as opposed to that of the relatively general referent of the predicate term.

My essay takes a simpler approach. I assume some prior identity between deconstruction and negative theology, in order to show *that* and *why* deconstruction cannot be subsumed under negative theology. According to Derrida, negative theology is inscribed within the dominant logocentric structure of metaphysics. Its principle is the irreducibility and reciprocity of unity and plurality, identity and difference. Derrida, however, claims to write otherwise than metaphysically. The ultimate principle of this writing is *différance,* which is different from the principle of identity and different even from itself. It is precisely the refusal of identity that makes deconstruction something different from negative theology. I try to show how deconstruction's refusal of identity successfully enables it to escape understanding. How so?

To understand another's discourse always implies a deep common accord based on identity. Understanding proceeds with the "good will" of hermeneutics by which it establishes an ethical relationship with the voice of the text. Hermeneutics is committed to submit its understanding to the text to show the bonds of agreement. Derrida's text, however, denies that it can be understood; it rejects the presumed identity between reader and text, which is a condition of understanding. What is logically impossible is in some sense ethically possible when the "good will" committed to respecting the voice of the other meets an arbitrary refusal of mutual recognition.

What is at stake here? To many readers of Derrida, it is not clear how deconstruction can be justified. On what grounds can deconstruction, either as method or doctrine, claim legitimacy? If deconstruction wills to reject any grounds of validity, and is always nonetheless parasitic toward them, does it show us an admirable capacity to "live" with contradiction, or is it necessarily a dangerous and nihilistic practice?

The question of deconstruction's legitimacy comes together

with the suggestion that Derrida can be read as a kind of crypto-theologian. Derrida's ambivalence toward the suggestion that deconstruction is a kind of negative theology (such that even his denials can be taken by his readers as affirming the connection) helps the cause of legitimating deconstruction. One could reason in this way: If negative theology is in fact a necessary element within the whole of systematic theological reflection, and deconstruction is a kind of negative theology, then deconstruction is not merely a rhetorical technique but part of a legitimate moment in systematic theological reflection. Seen in this light, one might embrace deconstruction on the grounds that Derrida is a crypto-theologian, a Pseudo-Dionyius of our time.

My intention was to inquire whether or not one can justify deconstruction by appealing to negative theology as its ground of legitimacy. The answer is no, because deconstruction is committed to rejecting the very logic of judgment that would make either an affirmation or negation possible. Deconstruction wills not to affirm any ground or goal of its practice. It intends to be different, but not "for the sake of anything" it or anyone else can articulate.

Scharlemann's second question concerns the "open secret of negative theology," namely, that meditation on the name of God opens a way to God in language. I suggest that this open secret seems to be known to Derrida: his *différance* likewise inscribes an open space. But Scharlemann finds unclear my elucidation of the mystical ascent through the names in Pseudo-Dionysius. He asks me what it means to say that "the hyperessential God . . . takes place when attention to the openness withdraws and gives way to divine darkness"? And he asks in what sense is "God" a name?

Scharlemann himself gives an interpretation of what is meant by "divine darkness" with the negative notion of "lack of appropriability." Let me supplement Scharlemann's suggestion with a positive notion: the hyperessential God occurs when the agency of my thinking about the openness of thinking and being shifts from my "I" as origin point of the thinking to the openness itself. "I" am still thinking, but no longer as sole agent of thinking; I am also being thought by a quasi agency manifest and hidden in the openness itself. My attending to the openness of thinking and being withdraws behind an agency which is not mine and remains concealed (hence the image of darkness) and yet sustains my own thinking.

I have in mind here the kind of transformation of thinking recorded by Heidegger's language of "thinking as thanking." In this case, a countervailing presence breaks into the activity of critical reflection (which on its own can come to think the openness of thinking being). This divine presence appears only in the thinking, and it enables the thinker to think more than the sheer openness by thinking in response to that which is absolutely other than that openness. I'll try to be more precise.

In thinking the "openness" by thinking my thinking of being, I posit being as that to which my thinking is necessarily directed. I posit being on the basis of my thinking. In responding to what is still other than that openness of thinking to being, an absolute otherness ("divine darkness" in relation to thinking), thinking responds intuitively to the realness of the real beyond the structure of thinking about being. That is, one might have an intuition of God beyond being. Naturally one can only think about this divine presence in its absence, for during the experience one is both thinking and being thought. When the element of being thought is gone, and one is only thinking about the openness of thinking to being, the divine presence is no longer around. The possibility of such an experience of a divine presence (denoted "divine darkness") resides in the divine name. Words or names as both thoughts and things can mediate the mind's intending of reality and they can mediate the intuited presence of reality to the mind. Consider how the divine name "God" might work in this way.

Scharlemann points out that for Pseudo-Dionysius, the names of God are initially titles that can be predicated of God. My point is that in the paths of descent and ascent, Pseudo-Dionysius both affirms and negates various titles (or names) predicated of God so that the divine name ("God") itself might reveal a potentiality of divine self-manifestation beyond the logic of divine predication.

In the positive way, Pseudo-Dionysius uses both conceptual names and common names. The conceptual names do not assign a predicate to the subject "God" but rather indicate something of God's nature. The common names indicate of God that God is the cause of everything that is. In saying, for example, "God is Goodness," the proposition does not define the subject God as (in some sense) possessing the property of goodness (but in another sense not). Rather, the predicate mirrors the subject so as to disclose its truth: God's being is simply to be, it is the openness of thinking to being ("Goodness"). The negative way supplements the positive way by correcting its one-sidedness. By introducing the negations, Pseudo-Dionysius directs attention from the positive form of the speculative proposition to the self-manifesting power of the name.

In saying, for example, "God is not Goodness" Pseudo-Dionysius establishes the openness of thinking to being and denies that God is that openness. Through this proposition, the mind's attention runs from the conceptual name back to the proper name "God," not as title but as an instantiator working like the pronoun "I." This is one of the points at which Scharlemann's work on fundamental theological terms is illuminating. Scharlemann has shown how the proper name "God" can instantiate absolute otherness in the very act of saying or thinking the name. "God" manifests the universal subjectivity that is not-I and not-this and not-nothing. If so, the name "God" has the capacity to manifest a meaning and reality not thought in thinking the openness of thinking to being. I am claiming that the negative way in Pseudo-Dionysius makes use of the instantiating power of the name "God" to present the divine reality "beyond being" to understanding. That is the "open secret."

Scharlemann's third question concerns the way in which I posed the question whether Derrida's *différance* might be construed as a divine name. Scharlemann asks whether the question should perhaps read: "Is the practice of meditating on the divine names analogous to the writing of *différance*?" Yes, indeed. This formulation shows more clearly the common ground: both are ways of opening a place at which the unappropriable may appear.

Scharlemann is correct: I do suggest that the effort to interpret deconstruction as a form of negative theology cannot be carried through. Hermeneutics cannot appropriate deconstruction "as" negative theology or anything else, and deconstruction cannot cancel hermeneutics on its side. My point is as Scharlemann says: the two are in irreducible polarity. The "rhetorical reading" turns deconstruction back onto itself in an attempt to show the otherness of this irreducible polarity. This intention unfortunately conflicts with the point I make in note 27, as Scharlemann points out. Deconstruction cannot be taken as a replacement for the old ontotheology, but something different from it altogether.

Scharlemann's fourth question focuses on the final portion of my paper, where I show how hermeneutics and deconstruction both undergo a reversal when confronted by the other. I pose the possibility that God could be named as the overturning of the one by the other, that God could be named as the overturning. Scharlemann asks about the assertion that God "is God as . . ." in its difference from predicating names of God. Is the formulation that

"God is God as the overturning" a predication which catches the intention of traditional negative theology (that God "neither is nor is not . . ."), or does this formulation have another intention?

My sense is that I have blurred two distinct possibilities, namely, that of speaking first about the being of God as a symbol of divinity and second about the being of God as the final unity of opposites. If the "overturning" were a symbol of God with the capacity to present to mind the being of God while itself being "other" than God, then it would have been proper to write "God is God as the overturning." But given that the "overturning" relationship between hermeneutical reflection and deconstruction allows one to approximate a "seeing" or discerning of the final unity of being and nonbeing or identity and difference, rather than presenting a concrete symbol of God's otherness, I ought to have avoided the phrasing of "God is God as . . ." in favor of the suggestion that the "overturning" is a dynamical name of God, which incorporates in the name itself both the act of positing and the act of canceling that were part of traditional negative theology.

Finally, Scharlemann asks a question which arises between my essay and that of Wyschogrod about the difference between *différance* and the *chōra*. Under my account Derrida's *différance* names the place within which being and nonbeing can appear, whereas in Wyschogrod's account *chōra* names the place within which even *différance* appears. Scharlemann asks whether that way of putting it is correct. My answer is yes. One can find these relationships sketched out by Derrida himself in "Comment ne pas parler: dénégations."

MARK C. TAYLOR

ROBERT SCHARLEMANN'S response to "Think Naught" is remarkable *not* for what it says but for what it does *not* say. What has Scharlemann not thought, or, at least, not written? What has he left unthought? What has he thought naught? What withdraws from his thought? *Can* one think what Scharlemann has not thought? What he has left unthought? What he has thought naught? What withdraws from (his) thought?

Scharlemann has not thought the question of figure . . . or the absence of figure. He has, therefore, left figure unfigured. It is, of course, possible that this unfiguring figures the unfigurable. Possible, but not likely. "Think Naught" is, among other things, about the work of art—painting and its subtext, drawing. The essay explores the way in which visual art might figure what remains unfigured in the Western ontotheological tradition. And yet there is not a single word about painting or drawing in Scharlemann's response. "Stylistic features," he acknowledges, "are part of 'errancy'. . . . But," he continues, "I want to put them aside in order to pose some questions about the conceptual content of the essay." Style vs. content . . . figure vs. concept.

Scharlemann's dismissive gesture is not accidental, for it is not only characteristic but is actually definitive of ontotheology. Substance is separated from style as kernel from husk and wheat from chaff. Style is regarded as figurative embellishment that can, indeed, must be stripped away in order to reach the thing itself. From this point of view, the conceptual is essential and the figurative is mere appearance. From the time of Plato, philosophy has been suspicious of art. As the realm of semblance, art, it is argued, is both misleading and subversive. Since art appeals to the senses and emotions instead of reason, philosophy distrusts it. When Plato banished poets from his ideal city, he initiated a long tradition of repressing or dismissing art. This rejection, which need not be explicit, is often indirect—as when Scharlemann ignores rather than engages the question of art. From the perspective of ontotheology, the task of philosophy is to translate figures and images into concepts and ideas. In this way, the philosopher prepares the way for the kingdom of reason in which every trace of sense will be erased.

But the repressed does not go away; it *withdraws* and waits for

the moment when it can return. To think beyond the end of theology, it is necessary to think this withdrawal. From what does
reason withdraw? What withdraws from reason? The question of
a/theology becomes: How can withdrawal be thought? If the ontotheological tradition is constructed by repressing figuration, then
it might be possible to think withdrawal by refiguring figure with
drawing. This refiguring would deconstruct the edifice of Western
philosophy and theology.

Drawing underlies painting. Though it appears superficial, painting is profound. Appearance and depth mingle on a surface that
is incalculably complex. Painting figures even when it disfigures
or is nonrepresentational, and disfigures even when it is figurative or representational. The play of figuring and disfiguring—both
within and beyond painting—is inescapable and endless. Painting
marks and mars the surface it inscribes. "To paint" derives from
the Latin *pingere* (to paint, to draw, embroider, or tattoo), whose
stem is *peig*, which means to cut, mark (by incision). To paint
is, then, to (dis)figure. Painting marks and mars the surface it inscribes by cutting and incising, tearing and rending. In the work
of art, rending rends and rendering is always already rent.

In Greek, "paint" is rendered *pharmakon*. "The seed of life"
and "the seed of death," a gift that is *ein Gift*, "the *pharmakon*
is ambivalent, . . . it constitutes the medium in which opposites
are opposed, the movement and the play that links them among
themselves, reverses them or makes one side cross over into the
other. . . . The *pharmakon* is the movement, the locus, and the
play: (the production of) difference. It is the differance of difference. It holds in reserve, in its undecided shadow and vigil, the
opposites and the differences that the process of discrimination
will come to carve out."[1] In this carving and cutting, painting is
never simply itself, but is always a trace of another trace. The trace
that is the condition of the possibility of painting is drawing. But
what is drawing? What is a drawing? What does it mean to draw?
What is a draw? There are not simple answers to these questions,
for *draw* and *drawing* are extraordinarily complex words. To appreciate the enigma of figuring and disfiguring, it is not necessary
to think *about* drawing but to think *with* drawing.

It is difficult to know where to begin or to end. To draw, which
derives from *dhragh* (to draw, drag on the ground), means, among
other things—many other things: to pull, drag, contract, shrink,
distort; to pull (a curtain, veil, etc.) over something to conceal it;
to pull (a curtain, veil, etc.) away from something to reveal it; to

render into another language or style of writing, translate; to bear, endure, suffer, undergo; to adduce, bring forward; to turn aside, pervert; to add, subtract, multiply; to attract by physical or moral force; to pull out, extract; to deduce, infer; to select by lot; to cause to flow; to take in (air, etc.), breathe; to take out, receive, obtain (money, salary, revenues) from a source; to empty, drain, exhaust, deplete; to stretch, extend, elongate, spin (a thread); to straighten out by pulling; to represent, mould, model; to frame; to compose; to track (game by scent); to trace (a figure) by drawing a pencil, pen, or the like across the surface; to cut a furrow by drawing a plow-share through the soil; to draw a line to determine or define the limit between two things or groups; to lay down a definite limit of action beyond which one refuses to go; to pull or tear in pieces, asunder; to bring together, gather, collect, assemble; to leave un-decided (a battle or game) . . . *Drawing* is irreducibly duplicitous. Its meaning cannot be pinned down, for it is constantly shifting and changing between opposites it neither unites nor divides: dis-torting / straightening, adding / subtracting, taking in / taking out, bringing forward / turning aside, revealing / concealing, gather-ing together / tearing asunder. The meaning of *draw(ing)* remains forever undecided. In this word, meaning itself is a draw.

Though the meaning of *drawing* is undecidable, its oscillation and alternation involve a rhythm that suggests "the origin of the work of art." This "origin" is not a foundation or ground but is an abyss or *Ungrund*, which never appears as such but "appears" only by withdrawing. When withdrawing is figured with drawing, it ap-pears to be the appearance of disappearance. As a rend(er)ing that simultaneously opens and closes, drawing marks and remarks the opening or clearing in which figures appear and disappear. "And yet—beyond what is, not away from it but before it, there is an other that occurs. In the midst of beings as a whole, there is an open place. This is a clearing, a lighting. Thought of in relation to what is, to beings, this clearing is in a greater degree than are beings. This open center, therefore, is not surrounded by what is; rather, the lighting middle itself encircles all that is, like the nothing we hardly know.[2]

"The nothing we hardly know" withdraws. The "with" of draw-ing is a strange with. Drawing not only joins and gathers but also tears and sunders. The work of art is not to reconcile opposites but to articulate differences. Articulation is a separating that gathers and a gathering that separates. Neither movement can be reduced to the other. Drawing de-fines the limit that neither joins nor separates whatever exists or does not exist.

To be drawn into the draw of drawing—to linger in the draw with drawing rather than repressing or dismissing it—is to be drawn to a void that cannot be a-voided. This void "is" no more emptiness than it is fullness, no more nothing than it is being. It *neither* is *nor* is not. Not absent without being present, it is a "nonabsent absence." The nonabsent absence of the void eludes the economy of ontotheology. Its chief asset—and its primary liability—is its withdrawal. Though speculation seeks a return on every invest-ment, there are losses that cannot be calculated, expenditures that promise no return. The incalculable cannot be figured.

The unfigurable withdraws from thought. Thought cannot think this withdrawal. Nor can it avoid thinking it. In a certain sense, thought thinks a withdrawal that is not its own by *not* thinking it. This withdrawal, which is not *of* thought, is what Scharlemann has not thought. Or, perhaps, *malgré lui*, has thought by not think-ing, which is not the same as thinking not. Scharlemann seems to want me to want that which withdraws from thought to be One, if not identity, to be divine, if not God. But it is not. It "is" not. To figure the unfigurable with drawing instead of with concepts and ideas leaves one wanting. To attempt to disfigure the unfigurable by rendering that which withdraws from thought as One, God, or the divine is to withdraw withdrawing. But every such a-voidance fails, for withdrawal withdraws from all efforts to withdraw it. Withdrawal, in other words, is unavoidable. "It is the sacred itself that is lacking, wanting, failing or withdrawn. The lack of the sacred names is not a surface lack concealing *and* manifesting the depths of a sacred held in reserve. It bars the way to the sacred, the sacred as such no longer comes, and the divine is withdrawn from itself."[3] . . . Withdrawal . . . Abandonment . . . Desertion . . . incalculable, unfigurable, unavoidable withdrawal . . .

Have I answered Scharlemann's questions? I suspect not. But I have always suspected naught. Suspected not of something else, suspected naught of something other. Suspected naught of pre-cisely what I cannot say. But something else, something other. Perhaps I *have* answered Scharlemann's questions by not answer-ing them. But, if so, then, perhaps he *has* thought naught by not thinking withdrawing with drawing.

NOTES

1. Jacques Derrida, *Dissemination*, trans. Barbara Johnson (Chicago: Univ. of Chicago Press, 1981), p. 127.
2. Martin Heidegger, "The Origin of the Work of Art," trans. Albert Hofstadter (New York: Harper and Row, 1971), p. 53.
3. Jean-Luc Nancy, "Of Divine Places," *Paragraph* 7 (1986): 14.

EDITH WYSCHOGROD

ROBERT SCHARLEMANN has summarized my argument, both in its general drift and in detail, with great precision. Before turning to his specific queries, I should like to sketch the conceptual backdrop against which I believe they should be addressed. Scharlemann's questions focus the issues that arise when negation migrates so that it cannot be pinpointed as theological, interpretive, or ethical. This fluidity of the contexts in which negation figures—or, in deconstructive terms, dis-figures—distinguishes this realignment of discourses or concept-constellations in the work of Derrida and Levinas.

Despite the repudiation of the Enlightenment in much recent French thought, integral to these new formations is a certain inheritance of Enlightenment rationality. It reappears in the language of negation as if effaced or, in Derrida's terms, under erasure. Thus, for example, God-talk for Levinas is not theological but a new discourse, an ethical-theologistics, so to speak, and Derrida's deconstructive analyses of traditional negative theology, a linguistic / interpretational-theologistics. The Enlightenment emphasis on ethics and the epistemological subject cannot simply be extruded from theology but remains a subversive question: How can the "subject," no longer the rational subject of cognition, pure consciousness or the autonomous ethical actor reenter theological thinking?

Why, it might be asked, if Enlightenment reason is a target of deconstruction and ethics in Levinas's sense should it reappear not as it was, to be sure, but as effaced? The answer is to be found in the pragmatics of deconstruction: fear that a total extirpation either of singularity or of an axiological point of reference would, for Derrida, legitimate any and all textual interpretation, a conclusion already drawn by some deconstructionists and, for Levinas, a descent into violence. If this is so, why not consider a Heideggerian solution to the problem of the subject of cognition such as the one worked out by Tillich? This tack would avoid a narrow construal of reason without sacrificing reason altogether.

It lies beyond the scope of these remarks to explore the relationship of Levinas and Derrida to Heidegger. It must suffice for my purposes here to notice that Heidegger's reading of philosophy's history is criticized by Derrida (paradoxically), not because Heidegger deviates from traditional ontology and notions of reason, but because Heidegger's philosophy of being remains too closely bound up with them. It is, in fact, the anarchic side of Heidegger that Derrida finds useful. By contrast, Levinas criticizes Heidegger for what he believes is the potential for violence when being is made thematic. If one thinks away the specificity of existents in their singularity, it is not, for Levinas, nothing that comes to the fore but undifferentiated being. Being thus understood is a kind of unboundedness prior to the emergence of a thinking subject and, as such, infrarational.

With this backdrop in mind, consider Scharlemann's first question about whether Levinas's thought is an amalgam of mystical theology's negative side and Buber's view of encounter. For Levinas both mysticism and encounter endanger what is fundamental to ethics, the otherness or alterity of other persons. The Other is a commanding presence who summons me to responsibility and who does so by virtue of being other. To lose myself in the Other, to blur the boundaries of self and Other, is to destroy—to use Kantian language—the formal principle of action and thus to contaminate the action itself. To merge with the divine Other or at least to obscure the distinction between self and the Other is, it is generally agreed, the purpose of mysticism both in its affective and cognitive dimensions. The Other in mysticism becomes a means to sacred ecstasy. In conformity with Kant's Enlightenment perspective, safeguarding the alterity of the Other for Levinas is tantamount to saying that the Other can never be a means toward an extrinsic end such as the change in one's religious affects promised by mysticism.

But could it not be argued at a deeper level—the one I presume Scharlemann intends—that Levinas's Other is actually a locus of ontological fullness somehow rendered accessible through negative description? If this is so, is there not a genuine parallel between Levinasian alterity and traditional negative theology? This assumption would, I think, constitute a real misreading of Levinas. Interpreting the Other as ontological plenitude is impossible *per hypothesi* because what is ethically compelling about the Other is that the Other exists as lack and destitution. If the Other is already constituted as lack, then whence the descriptive terms that are to be negated in depicting the Other? These terms would derive from the self as the point of reference. Is the self not thereby making the Other a foil for itself so that it rather than the Other becomes the pivot of ethics, an outcome that reverses the terms of Levinas's analysis and subverts its intention?

Nor should Levinas's account of the relation with the Other be identified with Buber's view of the relation between an I and a Thou. Commenting on Buber respectfully but critically, Levinas generally faults Buber for the reciprocal character of the I-Thou relation, for the parity of its poles, the I and the Thou. The Thou has no priority over the I so that the encounter is actually symmetrical and commutative. Therefore the I-Thou relation, Levinas contends, is really spectatorlike and therefore similar to the I-It relation. What is more, the space of intersubjectivity in Buber's philosophy of dialogue, the between, is not an ethical space. For Levinas, the topos of ethics is assymetrical: the Other is at a height in relation to the self ordering it to responsibility rather than, as in Buber, a flat plane in which alterity has no privileged position.

Levinas also criticizes Buber's account of truth because for Buber truth is a function of relation, that which comes to pass in the between of the I-Thou encounter. For Levinas, the between constituted in relation cannot be the discursive space of philosophical thought. If philosophical thinking is to occur, something individual must step out of relation to become a cognitive subject. Separateness from the world is the necessary precondition for cognition as well as for the reception of alterity. Humans cannot live exclusively in the rarefied air of ethics, for Levinas, just as for Buber the I-Thou must eventually give way to I-It.

The degree and form of Buber's Kantianism has been the subject of considerable debate. However it probably can be safely maintained that the segregation of the objectifying I from the I of genuine relation in Buber and the separation of the cognitive from the ethical subject in Levinas derive, however indirectly, from the Kantian distinction between the noumenal and phenomenal worlds. It should be added however that, for the later Levinas of *Autrement qu'être*, the ethical subject is the guarantor of the truth of her or his predicative utterances thus bringing philosophical discourse and ethics into a kind of functional complicity.

Scharlemann goes on to ask about the identification of metaphysics with speech. Derrida often takes as a starting point for analysis Heidegger's claims that the history of being unfolds as a progressive veiling of the difference between being and beings and that this ongoing obscuring of the ontological difference constitutes the history of metaphysics. For Derrida, this history is in bad faith, an important element of which is the effort to name this difference, to linguistically pinpoint the name that precedes naming, that makes naming possible, the breach into language before language. All names, Derrida thinks, are already metaphysical names, a point he makes over and over again in a variety of ways, especially in his by now celebrated essay, "Différance." There, as in "*Ousia* and *Gramme*" and elsewhere, it is made clear that language does not govern being—Derrida is not a linguistic determinist—but, to the contrary, metaphysical protocols precede language. Thus speech is always already determined by the norms of metaphysics.

But is Scharlemann not asking the straightforward question, "Is there not after all a difference between being and language, between metaphysics and speech?" Is it not one thing to say that speech reflects metaphysics and another to claim that speech can be identified with metaphysics? These questions belong in the context of Derrida's comments about the relation of language and metaphysics to what he calls texts. Derrida thinks of metaphysics as a text, this in a double sense: not only does metaphysics communicate itself in language, but the subject of metaphysics is itself a linguistic artifact. Does Derrida however not *deny* that he ever argued for pantextuality in the strong sense, for the view that there is nothing outside the text, no *hors texte*? The repudiation of language without ontology notwithstanding, Derrida appears to mean by this rejection only that, on pragmatic grounds, one is forced to accept the thesis of referentiality so that, in practice, everyday names like table or butterfly can be regarded as having existential import. In any case, metaphysics is not such a name but a text awaiting decipherment through the traces of its history as inscribed in language.

Scharlemann's next question about the difference between hyperessential and deconstructive negative theology is especially perplexing, in part because of the various settings—the thought of Dionysius, Eckhart, Heidegger, and Levinas to name a few—in which Derrida discusses God, being and negation. Scharlemann asks whether there is a deconstructive counterpart for negative theology's "God is unlimited" and whether this counterpart might be "God is neither limited nor unlimited." Before offering a direct answer, it may be useful to ponder Derrida's view of Heidegger's segregation of being and God. Derrida calls attention to Heidegger's claim that, were he (Heidegger) to write a theology, he would not use the word being because faith has no need of being. Yet Derrida sees that, for Heidegger, being is the dimension in which the disclosure of faith comes to pass. If this is so, talk of being is inescapable and, as Derrida asserts, Heidegger falls into the onto-theological trap he tries to avoid.

The task bequeathed to Derrida, if he is to speak theologically at all, must be to speak otherwise than ontologically, otherwise than within the confines of the logos of metaphysics. To do so is to transcend philosophy. But to speak from the place of philosophy's transcendence in Western thought is to speak apocalypti-cally. Although Derrida is often interpreted as a thinker of end time, in a Nietzschean if not in a traditional eschatological vein, he also draws back from the inner truth of apocalypse which, as nonphilosophical and beyond language, is the event of apocalypse itself. Thus Derrida both disavows and echoes Kant's fear of a pure apocalyptic gnosis when he writes that today one must be at once both "mystagogue" and "*Aufklärer*." His only recourse is to think somehow without thinking either ontologically or apocalyptically.

The move to an/ontological thought comes about through a rapprochement with Levinas who thinks both ethically and an/ontologically. For Levinas the starting point for theological inquiry is the trace or mark incised by the Other within ontology. Traces for Derrida and Levinas are not transparent toward anything, least of all towards a ground of being and thus cannot be symbols in Tillich's sense.

With the preceding considerations in mind, an answer to Scharlemann's question about whether the proposition "God is neither limited nor unlimited" is deconstructive can be attempted. I think it is safe to conclude that this proposition is not decon-structive. It is perhaps dialectical in that what might be expected to flow from it is a kind of *Aufhebung:* the assertion that God is beyond the polar oppositions limited / unlimited. It is not decon-structive because what is relevant for deconstruction is not the scope or inclusiveness of the sentence's predicate. That is to say, the idea that the predicate "not limited nor unlimited" is broader somehow, that it excludes more widely than the predicate of tra-ditional negative theology which stipulates only that God is "not limited," is an irrelevant consideration. Instead, for deconstruc-tion, it is the subject term "God" and the copula (is) that must be placed in question. These terms are to be construed as in exile, migratory and errant, under erasure but also as continuing to re-verberate in the text of metaphysics and speech.

Next Scharlemann asks whether the "always already" in Der-rida is like Augustine's "now." Is it also different from the "now" in its flowing temporality? Perhaps the best equivalent in Augustine is not the present with the various paradoxes it generates, but the "before" of Augustine's "before creation," a notion so perilous, that Augustine simply refuses to think it. Creation constitutes an absolute beginning before which there is only the abyss-al divine nature. Despite repeated discussions of present time, Derrida's "always already" is, I think, bound up with the problem of the now only secondarily but primarily is to be linked with the temporality of an absolute beginning or origin.

The modern form of the problem of the beginning is first articulated in Kierkegaard's reflections on the time scheme of incarnation. "What could it mean to say that eternity enters into time," Kierkegaard asks. The eternal always existed and so must always have been in time. And yet if it is *time* that the eternal enters, then the eternal must have done so at some specific moment. But—and the cycle can only repeat itself—as eternal, it is always already in time, and so on. The issue for Derrida is not that of the Augustinian *nunc stans* nor of endless flux but how to think beginning, to conceive an Ur-origin that cannot be thought. Such an origin is a nonorigin, displaced, always already before and after the fact.

Scharlemann then asks about the relation of God's speech to human speech. The matter of whether divine and human speech can or cannot coincide is not, for Derrida, an "ultimate" question because both kinds of speech lie within a common framework, are bound by the same conventions. The polarities for Derrida are not divine / human but speech / writing where writing is understood as the repressed infrastructure of language, as what is excluded from it. The question of writing opens a range of problems too vast to consider here. Suffice it to say that writing cannot be identified with speech because speech—all speech—is already marked by metaphysics. Writing sets limits upon the ideality of speech, both divine and human, without itself being a limit concept. Unless of course divine speech could somehow be identified with writing but, in that case, the Holy Spirit as the *viva vox* and the scriptic God would be altogether different. But then perhaps to think this difference becomes the next task for a theology of writing.

On the question of the primordiality of the *chōra*, it indeed appears to dis-place *différance* in Derrida's recent work. As the place where *différance* appears, the *chōra* is somehow prior to *différance* in a sense hard to specify as Scharlemann suggests.

JANE MARY TRAU

PROFESSOR SCHARLEMANN'S comments pose a fundamental question concerning trinitarian dogma: Why three, and only three, persons? My explanation of the Trinity by way of Rahner's theology of the symbol focuses upon the logically prior problem for trinitarian doctrine: how can there be three yet one? This discussion does inevitably lead to Scharlemann's question, for once the three persons are understood as genuine symbols of the divine being, it is logical to inquire why *three* symbols of the divine? One may further ask, since God is by nature expressive, is not everything, all of creation, a genuine symbol of the divine? I am grateful to Professor Scharlemann, for the suggestions he proposes provide some promising pathways for further discussion.

Before I consider Professor Scharlemann's suggestions, let me affirm my belief in the inherent limitation of our endeavor. Though a philosopher by trade and a Christian by belief I, like many Christian philosophers, stand in awe of the audacious task at hand. I should say that I do not claim to "explain" the mystery of the revelation of Christ Jesus, but attempt to encounter that truth within the human understanding. It is appropriate that my discussion appear in an anthology on negation and theology, for I accept the claim that though we do experience God, we do not and cannot know the fullness of God's nature and will. We can know something of God, for God invites us into a relationship, and relationships require mutual self disclosure. At the same time, the Divine Being is beyond our total intellectual comprehension. It is in this spirit of wonder and awe that theologians and philosophers attempt to create bridges to the Ultimate Transcendent Reality, tentative artifacts of abstract concepts constructed as conveyances to a greater reality. We persist, however, for every now and then these wispy connections carry us across a misty and mysterious ravine, and provide glimmers and hints of that greater Reality.

Scharlemann offers two paths of discovery for the solution to the question, Why just three symbols of the one God? The first solution "derive(s) the threeness from the unity of genus, species, and individual in anything real; the other is to derive the threeness from the identity and difference of being and not being." A com-

Figure 1. The Fullness of the Real

Ground of being	Genus	Father (*fons et origo*)
Essential form	Species	Son (Logos)
Accidental appearance	Individual	Spirit

bination of these two approaches provides an interesting schema for solving the problem of threeness.

Let us begin with the fascinating analogy Scharlemann draws between the threeness of the Trinity and the unity of genus, species, and individual in any instance of actual being (fig. 1). Scharlemann proceeds from a particular (Aristotelean and Thomistic) description of the metaphysics of being: any actual object instantiates the ground of all being (genus as being qua being), a species (which gives being an essential form, i.e., a "way" of being), and the real individual, which is the unique actual reality existing as an instance of the species. For instance, in every human person we witness the genus of being, the species of humanity, and the particularity of this individual, say Mary or Joe. Assuming that one accepts this metaphysical framework, Scharlemann proposes that Father, Son, and Spirit, as genuine symbols of the Divine Being, each relates to the unity of genus, species, and individual that is present in every real existent, including God (see fig. 1). I see two problems with this account.

First, it places the symbol of "Father" at the level of genus, which could imply a superiority of the symbol of Father, and lead us back to the heresy of Subordinationism.[1] More importantly, it clashes with my case for Father as symbol. In my schema, the Divine Being is genus that expresses itself as Father (fig. 2). If Father is placed at the level of genus (as in fig. 1), Father stands as the primordial unity which is expressed, rather than as the expression of that primordial unity.

A second problem with Scharlemann's schema (fig. 1), is that it "demotes" Spirit to the level of accidental being. This cannot be the proper sphere of a symbol that is truly divine, for "accidental" nature clashes with divinity. It is true that in the human person of Jesus the Christ his human nature is accidental. This union of

Figure 2. The Three Divine Symbols

Ground of being	Genus	God
		(Divine being)
Essential form	Species	Father
		Son
		Spirit
Accidental appearance	Individual	Creatures and nature

full humanity with full divinity is the Incarnational mystery. Traditional Christian dogma has never claimed that Spirit per se is *both* human (or material, hence accidental) and divine. The Spirit may appear in the material world, but it is not itself accidental in any sense. Rather, the Spirit visits or dwells within accidental beings. Hence, it cannot be conceived as occupying the level of accidental appearance as depicted in figure 1.

To preserve the philosophical point I have made, that Divine Being is one and one only, we must reserve the position of genus for Divine Being alone. The three modes of symbolic expression occupy the status of species, for they are the three essential forms of Divine Being as symbolic expression (fig. 2). Because they are symbols of the divine, and therefore themselves divine, they are rightly species because they, and they alone, are the beings who are symbols and are also divine. At this point we are faced with Scharlemann's question: Why only three divine symbols. This may be answered by Scharlemann's second tack: the paradox of the ontology of the symbol.

The symbol is what it is not: the genuine symbol is distinct but not separate from that which it represents. In the case of the three divine symbols, Divine Being is the one being that is genus and species in itself. Hence, in figure 2 first and second *ousia* might rightly appear at the level of genus. As Scharlemann proposes, the symbolic expression of God as Father reveals God as being God. The symbolic expression of Jesus as God who is at once human and God, reveals the reality of being God and not being God. The symbolic expression of God as Spirit, "is the living mediation of being and not being God in the one who is named deity." Thus, the three divine symbols express the unity of being and not being in the Divine Reality, rather than the expression of the unity of genus, species and individual.

The assignment of Spirit to the level of species (fig. 2), rather than individual (fig. 1), leaves that category occupied by truly accidental or contingent individuals, creatures and nature. This schema allows to say that creatures and nature are indeed symbolic expressions of the Divine Being, but are *essentially* different from the three Divine Symbols precisely because they are individuals, that is, material particulars. Thus, pantheism is avoided and divine immanence is maintained. We can further say that the Spirit mediates not only between Father and Son but between genus and individual, and between species and individual, without making the mistake of assigning Spirit to that category. Referring to figure 2, Jesus as Logos occupies the level of species, and as Jesus of Nazareth occupies the level of individual. This dual ontological status is the mystery of the Incarnation. We can attempt to express this phenomenon as the paradoxical union of being and not being, made possible by the mediation of Spirit between these two modes of existence.

In sum, the Divine Being is its own first and second *ousia;* it is both genus and species because it is the only singular existent that instantiates the genus of Divinity. The Divine Specific Forms (Father, Son, and Spirit) are genuine symbolic realities of the Divine Being, and each is divine because of the reality it represents. Genuine individual beings have the status of first *ousia,* so genuine symbols cannot be themselves first *ousia.* For this reason, Spirit must remain at the level of species in Scharlemann's conceptual framework (as executed in fig. 2); and Jesus of Nazareth, the Christ, occupies both specific and individual status. Thus, he is both genuine symbol and first *ousia.*

The Incarnation, the very life of Jesus Christ, affirms that seeming contradiction at the heart of God's revelation. Victory by death and deliverance through destruction are paradigmatic paradoxes. The salvation story of Israel in the Hebrew Scriptures is further witness to the persistent presence of paradox in divine revelation. In our individual histories, accepting the reality of paradox is an essential spiritual truth and a pastoral necessity. The ontology of the symbol is a philosophical apprehension of this truth, that in the unity of being and nonbeing the intellect penetrates the given and grasps a greater transcendent reality. That paradox is an inescapable element of Christian faith is confirmed by the words of Saint Paul in 1 Corinthians 1:21–25.

Since in God's wisdom the world did not come to know him through "wisdom," it pleased God to save those who believe through the absurdity of the preaching of the gospel. Yes, Jews demand "signs" and Greeks look for "wisdom," but we preach Christ crucified—a stumbling block to Jews, and an absurdity to Gentiles: but to those who are called, Jews and Greeks alike, Christ the power of God and the wisdom of God. For God's folly is wiser than men, and his weakness more powerful than man.[2]

To believe in Christ is to believe in an absurdity, by human standards of reason. The doctrine of the Trinity is also absurd, for who can make sense of one that is three and three that are one? The paradoxical nature of the genuine symbol is thus an appropriate model for our attempt to grasp a glimmer of the true nature of the Divine Being. If we are correct in our understanding of divine revelation, that the doctrine of the Trinity reflects the true nature of God, then our description of the unity of being and nonbeing mediated by Spirit, makes that revealed truth accessible to reason.

NOTES

1. The use of exclusively male imagery in religious language is a vital topic for discussion. It is, however, tangential to our present concern. I have argued elsewhere ("Consequences of Exclusively Male Imagery in Religious Language," forthcoming in *Worship*) that masculine imagery is alone insufficient to provide fruitful images of God, and has negative consequences for women in social and ecclesial institutions. Realizing, however, that this is far from settled in philosophical and theological circles, I beg the reader's indulgence for this work, so that my comments concerning the traditional Christian doctrine not be complicated by secondary arguments and challenges.
2. *The New American Bible* (Nashville: Thomas Nelson, 1971).

DUE TO the limitation of my understanding, Scharlemann's discussion and questions concerning my essay are not necessarily clear to me. In the following, I will try to reformulate his discussion into two issues for clarification. First, Scharlemann states, "It might be argued that the polarity of being and nonbeing in Tillich's ontological structure is not meant to be the same as the polarity of being and nothing" in Buddhism. He also points out that "there seems to be a clear difference in the predications being made" in these two cases. So far, I understand that Scharlemann agrees with me in making a distinction between God and sunyata in terms of being and nothingness. However, in this connection we must clarify what that difference really means and what is the cause of the difference. These are crucial points of the present discussion.

Second, assuming that they—the polarity of being and nonbeing in Tillich and the polarity of being and nothing in Buddhism— are the same and that some theologian were to understand "God" to mean one who "is neither being nor nothingness and yet both being and nothingness," Scharlemann raises a question: "Would the names 'God' and 'sunyata' then be equivalent in meaning?"

In order to elucidate these issues properly I would like to clarify the following six points.

(1) The polarity of being and nonbeing in Tillich's ontological structure and the polarity of being and nothing in Buddhism are categorically different in their nature and role. In Tillich's ontological structure, as seen in his words "Being precedes nonbeing in ontological validity, as the word 'nonbeing' itself indicates" and "being 'embraces' itself and nonbeing," while "nonbeing is dependent on the being it negates. 'Dependent' points first of all to the ontological priority of being over nonbeing."[1] Nonbeing is understood to be ontologically subordinate to being. By contrast, in Buddhism "nothing" is not subordinate to being, but being and nothingness are understood to be of completely equal force in relation to each other. As I state elsewhere, "They [being and nothingness] are entirely relative, complementary, and reciprocal, one being impossible without the other. In other words, mu (nothing) is not one-sidedly derived through negation of u (being). Mu (nothing) is the negation of u (being) and vice versa. One has no logical or onto-

logical priority to the other. Being the complete counter-concept to *u* (being), *mu* (nothing) is more than privation of *u* (being), a stronger form of negativity than 'nonbeing' as understood in the West."[2] Accordingly, the term *nonbeing* cannot be properly used in Buddhism to indicate the negative side of reality. In order to indicate the negative side of reality, the terms *nothing* or *nothingness* are more appropriate in Buddhism. Thus we must know that, although equally indicating polarity, the polarity of being and nonbeing in Tillich and the polarity of being and nothing in Buddhism are essentially different from each other; the former is an asymmetrical polarity whereas the latter a symmetrical polarity.

(2) The Christian notion of God indicates the ultimate reality beyond the polarity and opposition of being and nonbeing, whereas the Buddhist notion of sunyata refers to the ultimate reality equally beyond the polarity and opposition of being and nothing. So far there is a sort of parallel between the two religions. However, since the nature of the polarity of positive and negative principle in these two religions is categorically different, the nature of the ultimate reality (God and sunyata) to be realized by overcoming that polarity is also essentially different. In Tillich, God is conceived as being-itself, and "being 'embraces' itself and nonbeing. Being has nonbeing 'within' itself as that which is eternally present and eternally overcome in the process of the divine life."[3] God does not exclude nonbeing but indicates a sort of dialectical relation of being and nonbeing. To use the term of Scharlemann, God is a "third in which being and nonbeing are united" or fused.

By contrast, in Buddhism the ultimate reality is realized as sunyata, which is not being-itself nor absolute Being but absolute nothingness. However, the absolute nothingness is not negative or nihilistic but most positive and dynamic. For sunyata, another term for absolute nothingness, is beyond the *symmetrical* polarity and opposition of being and nothing and thereby embraces being and nothing in their polarity and opposition. Unlike God, who— to use Scharlemann's phrasing of Tillich—"is" being-itself and "is not" nothing, sunyata "is" and "is not" being and "is" and "is not" nothingness.

(3) This difference between God and sunyata is not a difference in degree but in quality. The polarity of being and nonbeing in Tillich is based on being, as we see in his words "Being embraces itself and nonbeing." On the other hand, the polarity of being and nothing in Buddhism is based neither on being nor on nothing in their relative sense but upon absolute nothingness, that is, nothingness in

the absolute sense. Although we equally see polarity of being and nothing in both Tillich and Buddhism, the basis of polarity is radically different. In Tillich the ultimate reality (God) is conceived as the third in which being and nonbeing are united, whereas in Buddhism the ultimate reality (sunyata) is not the third nor the first nor the second. This means that in Buddhism ultimate reality is realized through the complete turning over of the original horizon of the polarity of being and nothing. In other words, not only the complete negation of nothing but also the complete negation of being; that is, the double negation of two poles is necessary for the realization of ultimate reality as emptiness.[4]

(4) This qualitative or categorical difference in the nature of polarity of being and nothing in Tillich and Buddhism indicates the different role of the polarity in attaining the ultimate reality in the religions. In Tillich, since the polarity of being and nothing is an asymmetrical polarity with being's superiority over nothing, the overcoming of this asymmetrical polarity leads us *obliquely* on the side of being to reach the ultimate point of being, that is, Being or being-itself. By contrast, in Buddhism, since the polarity of being and nothing is a symmetrical polarity, with equal weight for being and nonbeing, the overcoming of this symmetrical polarity entails us *straightforwardly* to go beyond the horizon of polarity itself to attain a new horizon which is neither being nor nothing—that is, to a realization of sunyata.

However, if sunyata is simply regarded as the end or goal of straightforward transcendence, it is neither true sunyata nor true emptiness because it is objectified and reified as the end. The objectified or reified emptiness is not true emptiness. Emptiness must be emptied. Transcendence must be transcended. True emptiness is the ever self-emptying activity that is incessantly turning into being. Thus true Emptiness is neither being nor nothing, and both being and nothing at one and the same time. This is why true Emptiness is called Wondrous Being.

This true Emptiness and Wondrous Being is the ultimate reality in Buddhism, which is realized only by transcending straightforwardly the horizon of polarity of being and nothing (and by returning to the original plane through transcending the transcendence). This straightforward transcendence is possible because the polarity of being and nothing is realized not as asymmetrical with being's superiority over nothing but as symmetrical, with equal weight of being and nothing. This means that in Tillich the polarity of being and nonbeing plays a role as the springboard for slantwise transcendence, whereas in Buddhism the polarity of

REPLIES   145

being and nothingness plays a role as the springboard for straightforward transcendence.

(5) When Tillich conceives God as the dialectical relation of
being and nonbeing, he indicates that God as the power of being
overcomes the shock of nonbeing, conquers nonbeing, and finally
fulfills being itself. Although this understanding of the relation of
being and nonbeing is dialectic, is not the whole dialectical movement taking place within the framework of being? It is true that in
The Courage to Be Tillich emphasizes that nonbeing opens up the
divine self-seclusion: "Nonbeing (that in God which makes his
self-affirmation dynamic) opens up the divine self-seclusion and
reveals him as power and love. Nonbeing makes God a living God.
Without the No he has to overcome in himself and in his creature,
the divine Yes to himself would be lifeless." Here we can see that
in Tillich the divine self-seclusion (the framework of being itself)
is opened up through the dialectical movement of nonbeing. In this
understanding, however, is the divine self-seclusion *completely*
opened up, and is the framework of being itself *fundamentally*
broken through? To answer these questions it would be helpful
to look at another quotation from *The Courage to Be:* "We could
not even think 'being' without a double negation: being must be
thought as the negation of the negation of being. This is why we
describe being best by the metaphor 'power of being.' Power is the
possibility a being has to actualize itself against the resistance of
other beings. If we speak of the power of being-itself we indicate
that being affirms itself against nonbeing."[5]

In this passage Tillich clearly talks about a double negation and
stresses that "being must be thought as the negation of the negation of being." However, from his theological stance can he equally
stress "nothingness must be thought as the negation of the negation of nothingness"? Only when this statement is clearly realized
together with the state "Being must be thought as the negation of
the negation of being" is the double negation as the key factor to
attain the ultimate reality fully realized and the divine disclosure
completely opened up. Here in Tillich we still see a superiority
of being over nothingness. What is the ontological ground of this
persistent superiority of being over nothingness?

As Tillich suggests, double negation is necessary to attain ultimate reality. In order to attain ultimate reality not only double
negation concerning being (that is, being as the negation of the
negation of being), but also double negation concerning nothingness (that is, nothingness as the negation of the negation of nothingness) is necessary. In Tillich double negation concerning being

(that is, being as the negation of negation of being) is clearly realized, but double negation concerning nothing (nothingness as the negation of negation of nothingness) is lacking. This is the reason why, to Tillich, ultimate reality is God as being itself or the power of being.

On the other hand, in Mahayana Buddhism double negation is carried out thoroughly to the extent that the horizon of the polarity of being and nothingness itself is overcome. In Mayahana Buddhism not only double negation concerning being—being as the negation of the negation of being—but also double negation concerning nothingness—nothingness as the negation of the negation of nothingness—is clearly realized. For instance, *Mula-Madhyamika Karitas* (13:7–8), an important writing of the Madyamika School, emphasizes that "Emptiness too is empty," and "sunyata—sunyata," and "Emptiness—emptiness" is stressed. These phrases indicate that emptiness must be negated to attain true Emptiness. This true Emptiness as the negation of emptiness is ultimate reality in Buddhism because this true Emptiness is nothing but Wondrous Being and true fullness. In order to attain Wondrous Being (absolute being), the double negation of being and nothingness is essential. Here the divine seclusion is completely opened up.

As we see above in Tillich, although the relation of being and nonbeing is grasped quite dialectically and being is realized through the double negation of nonbeing, in the final analysis being is given priority over nonbeing and God is conceived as Being itself. This concept of God cannot be accepted by Buddhists as the ultimate reality because to a Buddhist the ultimate is the complete nondual dynamism that is neither being nor nothingness and yet both being and nothingness. This dynamism has been traditionally expressed as "whatever is form, that is emptiness, whatever is emptiness, that is form" (Heart Sutra) and "Samsara as it is is nirvana; nirvana as it is is samsara."[6]

(6) There is still another important point in understanding the difference between Tillich and Buddhism in terms of the polarity of being and nothing. In Tillich, the question of being is produced by the "shock of nonbeing." The shock of nonbeing is inescapable to human existence due to human finitude. "Finitude unites being with dialectical nonbeing. Man's finitude, or creatureliness, is unintelligible without the concept of dialectical nonbeing."[7]

To Tillich the existential awareness of nonbeing is anxiety, which can be overcome only through faith as the courage to be.

This is so because courage is the self-affirmation of being in spite of nonbeing. "Faith is the state of being grasped by the power of being-itself."[8] This is Tillich's solution of the basic anxiety innate in human existence. Here again we see that, although the relation of being and nonbeing is understood dialectically, being and nonbeing (nothingness) are not grasped as opposing each other in a contradictory manner but in a way in which nonbeing is subordinate to being. How can this subordination of nonbeing (nothingness) to being be ontologically validated? I well understand that the courage to be in Tillich, and faith and hope in Christianity, are entirely an existential and personal experience that is beyond the ontological dimension. But however existential and personal faith as the courage to be may be, it needs to be ontologically verified in our time, when the raison d'être of religion, Christianity and Buddhism included, is questioned by various forms of anti-religious ideologies such as scientism, Marxism, traditional Freudian psychoanalytic thought, and nihilism in the Nietzschean sense.[9] So my question, How can the subordination of nonbeing (nothingness) to being be ontologically validated? is not merely an ontological but an existential question essentially related to our religious life.

In Buddhism, on the other hand, the polarity of being and nothingness (not nonbeing) is grasped thoroughly dialectically in that being and nothingness are not only opposing but also contradictory with each other. Since being and nothingness, or, more broadly, positivity and negativity, are essentially different and antagonistic principles, they consist of a fundamental antinomy or an existential dilemma. Buddhism understands human existence as a self-contradictory existence. The realization of one's own self-contradictory existence is called great death, which is not death as a counterpart of life but death as a fundamental conflict between life and death as the two antagonistic principles. A Buddhist solution of the human problem is realized by breaking through great death and attaining nirvana, a blissful freedom from life and death.

In the above, I have tried to clarify how different the understanding of the polarity of being and nothing is between Tillich and Buddhism. Now I would like to deal briefly with the second issue raised by Scharlemann. That is to say, if the assumption is made that the polarity of being and nothing or nonbeing is understood in the same way in Tillich and Buddhism and that some theologian understands "God" as one who "is neither being nor nothingness and yet both being and nothingness," Scharlemann raises a question: "Would the names 'God' and 'sunyata' then be equivalent in meaning?"

My answer is yes. That which is neither being nor nothingness and yet both being and nothingness indicates ultimate reality, which is the unobjectifiable nondualistic dynamism transcending and yet embracing all existing conflict and opposition. The Buddhist notion of sunyata or Emptiness which is at the same time Fullness and thereby is called Wondrous Being, indicates the nondualistic dynamism. But we need not cling to the term *sunyata*. As I stated earlier, sunyata or Emptiness must be emptied. What is important is not the term *sunyata* but the ultimate reality indicated by it. If "God" indicates ultimate reality in the above dynamic sense, "God" and "sunyata" are perfectly equivalent in meaning. Although Tillich's interpretation of God as being does not, as discussed above, indicate the ultimate reality in the above sense, Christian tradition is not lacking in such a nondualistic dynamic interpretation of God. For instance, Dionysius the Areopagite characterized God as "dazzling darkness." God is dazzling and yet dark: God is dark and yet dazzling. This, however, does not mean that God is *half* dazzling and *half* dark but that God is *fully* dazzling and yet at the same time *fully* dark: *fully* dark and yet at the same time *fully* dazzling. This is because to Dionysius the Areopagite, God as the ultimate reality is precisely the unobjectifiable, nondualistic dynamism. To him God is neither dazzling nor dark and yet both dazzling and dark. "God" as dazzling darkness is equivalent to "sunyata" in which samsara as it is, is nirvana: nirvana as it is, is samsara.

NOTES

1. Tillich, *Systematic Theology*, 1:189; idem, *The Courage to Be*, pp. 34, 40.
2. Abe, *Zen and Western Thought*, p. 127.
3. Tillich, *The Courage to Be*, p. 34.
4. Abe, "Non-Being and *Mu*," in *Zen and Western Thought*, pp. 121–34; Tillich, *The Courage to Be*, p. 180.
5. Tillich, *The Courage to Be*, pp. 180, 179.
6. Mahā-samnipata-sutra Taisho 397 (in vol. 13).
7. Tillich, *Systematic Theology*, 1:189.
8. Tillich, *The Courage to Be*, p. 172.
9. Masao Abe, "Kenotic God and Dynamic Sunyata," in *The Emptying God: A Buddhist-Jewish-Christian Conversation*, ed. John Cobb and Chris Ives (Orbis Books, 1990), pp. 3–9.

CONTRIBUTORS

MASAO ABE, having taught Buddhism before his retirement at the Claremont School of Theology, now teaches as Professor of Philosophy at Purdue University and is the author of *Zen and Western Thought* and many other comparative studies of Buddhism and Western philosophy and theology.

LANGDON GILKEY is Professor Emeritus of Theology at the Divinity School of the University of Chicago. Among his books are *Maker of Heaven and Earth, Naming the Whirlwind: The Renewal of God-Language, Religion and the Scientific Future,* and *Reaping the Whirlwind: A Christian Interpretation of History.*

DAVID E. KLEMM is Associate Professor of Religion at the University of Iowa. He is the author of *The Hermeneutical Theory of Paul Ricoeur* and of the two-volume *Hermeneutical Inquiry.*

ROBERT P. SCHARLEMANN is Professor of Religious Studies at the University of Virginia. His recent publications include *Inscriptions and Reflections: Essays in Philosophical Theology* and *The Reason of Following: Christology and the Ecstatic I.*

MARK C. TAYLOR is Professor of Religion at Williams College. He has published, among other books, *Kierkegaard's Pseudonymous Authorship, Journeys to Selfhood: Hegel and Kierkegaard, Erring: A Postmodern A/Theology,* and, most recently, *Tears.*

JANE MARY TRAU is Associate Professor in the Department of Philosophy and Theology at Barry University. Her publications include *The Co-Existence of God and Evil.*

EDITH WYSHOGROD is Professor of Philosophy at Queens College of the City University of New York. Her published books include *Emmanuel Levinas: The Problem of Ethical Metaphysics, Spirit in Ashes: Hegel, Heidegger, and Man-Made Mass Death,* and *Saints and Postmodernism: Revisioning Moral Philosophy.*

INDEX

Abe, Masao, 82
Absence, 35, 123, 129
Absolute, 96
Abstraction, 31 f.; as method of
    negation, 28
Accidental, 138
Actual, and virtual, 45
Affirmation, 92
Alterity, 21, 132
Analogical predication, 3
Analogy, 12
Anselm, 9–11
Anxiety, 146 f.
Aphairesis, 28, 30
Apophasis, 2, 28, 30, 48
Apophatic, 41; *see also* Discourse,
    apophatic
Approaches to religion, 88
Aquinas, *see* Thomas Aquinas
Architecture, 38 n. 5
Art, 27, 126, 128
Aseity, 83
Autonomy, 3, 75, 81, 82, 83

Barth, Karl, 1, 8, 11, 88; on Anselm's
    proof, 10 f., 22 n. 5
Beginning, 25, 136
Being, 104; absolute, 82; and God,
    1, 3, 14, 134 f.; and nonbeing,
    6 f., 114, 117–19, 142 f.; and
    nothingness, 142 f., 145, 147;
    as being, 15; as copula, 135;
    as symbolic, 59 f.; asymmetri-
    cal polarity of, 92 f.; new, 79;
    openness of, 101; power of, 145;
    structure of, 6, 123; theonomous
    concept of, 83; ways of, 112 f.
Being-itself, 6, 83, 84, 96, 117 f.

Being like (being as), 100, 103 f.
Bergson, Henri, 42–44, 47, 49, 52 f.,
    106
Beyond being, 7, 15, 30
Black, 26; as presence of light, 29, 30
Black Paintings, *see* Reinhardt, Ad
Bonhoeffer, Dietrich, 93
Braga, Synod of, 58
Brahman, 96, 97
Brauer, Jerald, 87
Buber, Martin, 107, 133
Buddhahood, 88, 93
Buddhism, 6 f., 88; and Protestant
    principle, 88, 90; as neither dual-
    istic nor monistic, 97; principle
    of, 96 f.

Catholic substance and Protestant
    principle, 78
Causality, 15
Chōra, 46 f., 125; and *différance,* 136
Christology, 64
Color, absence and presence of, 29
Community, 84
Concupiscence, 77
Conversation, 5 f.
Coorigination, dependent (*pratitya
    samutpada*), 96 f., 117
Correlation, 74
Courage, 78, 146
Creation, 70, 136
Creatures, 140
Cross, 34, symbol of, 117
Cubism, 27, 38 n. 5

Deconstruction, 3, 9, 16, 20 f., 102,
    124; and language, 24 n. 33;
    and negative theology, 8, 12–14,

Deconstruction (*cont.*)
16, 102 f., 121, 135; and ontotheology, 24 n. 27; as rhetorical
technique, 122; as requiring
another, 17; as textual practice,
21 f.; hermeneutical reading of,
16 f.; justification of, 121; pragmatics of, 131; reversal of, 124;
rhetorical reading of 19 f.; syntax
of, 16
Deferral, 46
Deity, reality of, 114
Deleuze, Gilles, 42 ff.
Demonization, 89
Derrida, Jacques, 1, 5, 6, 8, 10 f., 15,
41, 100 f., 106; and John Searle,
41; and negative theology, 107 f.;
as theologian, 122; on No-saying,
54; rhetorical reading of, 17
Descombes, Vincent, 41, 45
Desire, 106
Dialectic and dialogue, 5–7
Différance, 6, 10–12, 15, 20, 21, 101
f., 125; and undecidability, 18; as
divine name, 15, 124; in relation
to *chōra*, 136; meaning of, 15 f.
Difference, 105; and refusal, 6; onto-
logical, 133; play of, 15, 34
Differing, 5–7
Dionysius the Areopagite, 2, 13, 19,
41, 47 f., 52, 100, 120–24, 148;
positive and negative ways of,
21 f.
Discernibility of individuals, 56
Discourse, apophatic, 12 f., 53;
christological, 68; negative, 51
Discrimination of nondiscrimina-
tion, 97 f.
Divine being, 66
Divine darkness, 122 f.
Docetism, 56
Doubt, 43
Drawing, 127 f.
Dualism, 44
Duration, 44
Dynamism, 46

Eckhart (Meister Eckhart), 19, 27, 41,
52
Einstein, Albert, 47
Eliade, Mircea, 86 f.
Emptiness, 35, 77, 91, 144, 146, 148;
see also Sunyata
Encomium, 18
End, 31
Enlightenment, 131 f.

Equality, 97
Erasure, 131
Esse ipsum, 1
Evil, radical, 85 n. 2
Existence, 147; as symbolic, 59;
modes of, 66
Expansion and contraction, 44
Experience, modern, 74
Expression, 60–63, 69 f.
Expressionism, 26 f.

Faith, 146 f.; justification by, 80
Feminist thought, 65 f.
Feuerbach, Ludwig, 82
Finality, 31
Finitude, 24 n. 4, 76, 78, 146; struc-
ture of, 78
Form, 31, 35
Formlessness, 31, 35, 82
Freedom, 3, 4, 43, 68, 75, 82; Kant
on, 3 f.; *see also* Autonomy
Fulfillment, 79

Gadamer, Hans-Georg, 13; on finitude, 24 n. 34
Genus, 109–14, 137 f.
God, 1, 3–5, 6 f., 14, 51, 72, 114, 115,
123, 143; absence of, 35; and
difference, 22; and freedom, 4;
and language, 14, 108; and "not"
or nothing, 1, 7, 83, 104; and
religion, 89; and sunyata, 92–
94, 143, 147 f.; Anselm on, 9 f.;
as ground of being, 75, 107 f.; as
openness of being and thinking,
123; as proper name, 123, 124;
as one, 105; as polarity of being
and nonbeing, 72, 85; as name,
101 f.; as overturning, 21, 124;
as power of being, 79, 83; as self-
sufficient, 84; as subject, 135; as
triune, 69 f.; as ultimate reality,
148; death of, 34; holiness of, 7;
identity in, 109 f.; in relation to
being, 134 f., 145; knowability
of, 62 f.; names of, 13 f.; ontological proof of, 10, 21; opposites
in, 148; otherness of, 15; positive and negative paths to, 13 f.;
predicates of, 4; presence of, 35;
revelation of, 10; theistic notion
of, 92, 93, 94; unity of persons
in, 69
God above God, 96
God-talk, in Levinas, 131
Good, metaphor of, 50

Good will, 16 f., 19; as will to power, 17 f.; of hermeneutics, 13
Grace, 78
Great death, 147

Hegel, G. W. F., 3, 82
Heidegger, Martin, 1, 19, 23 n. 12, 49, 73, 131 f.; Derrida's criticism of, 132; Levinas's criticism of, 132
Hermeneutics, 124; and deconstruction, 3, 9, 16 f., 20 f., 102, 103, 124; as textual practice, 21 f.; as will to power, 102; ethical relation in, 121; reversal of, 124
Heteronomy, 76
Holy, 88–90, 94
Hubris, 78
Hyperessentiality, 12
Hypostasis, 113

Idealism, 4
Identity, 70 n. 1, 83, 105, 111
Individual, 137 f.; in Trinity, 109–14
Individuality, 4
Instantiators, 14
Invocation, 108

Jerusalem, 18, 47–49
Jesus, 63, 66, 67, 95 f., 139 f.
Jiriki, 81, 82; *see also* Tariki

Kierkegaard, Søren, 35
Kyoto School (Buddhism), 72

Language, 11, 14, 40, 102
Levinas, Emmanuel, 42, 49–54; and Buber, 132 f.; on negative theology, 108
Light, 29
Love, 63

Meaning, God as power of, 79
Mediation, 81
Metanoesis, 80, 81
Metaphor, 107, 145
Metaphysics, 4, 53, 107, 121, 133; and ontology, 50; and speech, 113 f.; as text, 134; Bergsonian, 45 f.; infrastructure of, 53; of desire, 50
Method, 95; existential, 72–75; theological, 73
Mies van der Rohe, Ludwig, 28
Modalism, 57, 112 f.
Modernism, 27, 28
Monism, 44

Monotheism, 109; Trinity and, 57
Mu (nothing), 142
Mysticism, 93, 107, 132

Name, 14 f., 101, 123, 134
Naught, *see* Nothing
Negation, 28 f., 54, 131; absolute, 92; and affirmation, 92; and French philosophy, 41; as privative, 44; Bergson and Deleuze on, 42–45; deconstructive and negative, 107; double, 3–5, 35, 77, 88, 92, 97, 103, 105, 144, 145 f.; expressions of, 40; interpretations of, 42; kinds of, 2, 42, 108; language of, 43; Levinas on, 50; of discrimination, 97 f.; roots of, 42; strategies of, 32, 41
Negative theology, 2 f., 17, 23 n. 7, 27, 100 f., 107, 122; and deconstruction, 16; as textual practice, 12 f.; Derrida on, 8 f., 11 f., 16; origin of, 106; secret of, 13–15; senses of, 39 f.; types of, 108; *see also* Theology
Negativity, 13, 78, 80
New being, 78, 79
Newman, Barnett, 26
Nicholas of Cusa, 24 n. 18
Nietzsche, Friedrich, 73
Nirvana, 77, 88, 90, 116, 148; and great death, 147; and samsara, 93 f.; and sunyata, 91; as cessation of will, 77
Nishitani, Keiji, 72 f., 114
Nonbeing, 6 f., 43 f., 104, 115; as distinct from nothingness, 142; Tillich on, 7, 92; shock of, 78, 145; types of, 49; understanding of, 42
Nondiscrimination, 97
Nonobjectivism, 27
Nonsubstantiality, 93
Not, *see* Negation; Nothing
Nothing (nothingness), 1, 25, 49, 72, 74, 78, 79, 81, 82, 93, 115, 128, 143, 145, 146; and God, 84, 104; as divine, 35; as ground of reality, 72; ways of thinking of, 25, 104
Now, 108, 135
Nunc stans, 108, 136

Objectification, 97
Odysseus, 51
Ontotheology, 7, 37, 103, 124, 126,

Ontotheology (*cont.*)
    135; and deconstruction, 24
    n. 27; economy of, 30
Origen, 58
Orthodoxy, 88
Other, 50–52, 68, 70, 76, 79–83,
    106 f., 108, 115, 122, 129, 132 f.
Otherness, 6, 14, 20, 103, 123
Other Power, 81, 82, 84
Ousia, 111, 113, 139 f.; first, 113; first
    and second, 60 f., 112; meaning
    of, 57 f.
Overturning, 9; as predicate of God,
    103

Painting, 127
Pantheism, 140
Paradox, 61, 63, 140
Person, 68, 76
Persona, 112, 113; in God, 109; mean-
    ing of, 57 f.
Philosophy, French and English, 40 f.
Physis, 112, 113
Plato, 19, 41
Plenitude, 46
Polarity, 143 f.; basis of, 144; of being
    and nothingness, 147; symmetri-
    cal and asymmetrical, 143 f.
Possibility, 44 f.
Prayer, 52
Presence, 35, 123, 129; negative, 35
Property, 112
Prophecy, 51 f.
Prosōpon, 113
Providence, 79
Pseudo-Dionysius, *see* Dionysius the
    Areopagite
Pure Land, 73

Rahner, Karl, 59
Realism, 4
Reality, ordinary, 77; symbolic, 112 f.
Reinhardt, Ad, 26; Black Paintings of,
    27, 29 f., 35
Religion, 34; approaches to, 88; crite-
    rion of, 94 f., 96, 97; critique of,
    35; history of, 88 f., 94, 97, 116;
    inner aim of, 89; judging of, 96;
    of the concrete spirit (Tillich),
    89; sacramental basis of, 89;
    typology of, 88 f.
Religion of the concrete spirit, 93
Repetition, 25
Representation, 32; failure of, 27
Revelation, 95 f.

Reversal, 20, 35
Rilke, Rainer M., 54
Ritual, 94
Rothko, Mark, 26

Sabellianism, 57
Sacred, 36 f., 88, 92
Salvation, 77, 140; history of, 67
Samsara, 77, 88, 90, 116, 148
Schleiermacher, Friedrich, 84
Searle, John, 41
Secularity, 88, 89, 92 f.
Self, 74, 77, 78, 90, 115; and language,
    11; and no-self, 79; and world,
    78; as projection of desire, 77;
    as unity of pluralities, 59, 67;
    elements of, 84
Selfhood, 72
Sophistry, 19
Space, 47–49
Species, 137 f.
Species, in Trinity, 109–14
Speech, 136; and metaphysics, 113 f.;
    and violence, 53; apocalyptic,
    135; in polarity with writing,
    136; mystical, 47
Spinoza, Benedict, 3, 82
Spirit, theology of, 71 n. 17
Structure, ontological, 6 f.
Subordinationism, 65, 138
Substance, 111, 113
Sunyata, 72, 91, 97, 116, 118, 143,
    148; and religion 93 f.; and
    God, 118, 147 f.; compared with
    Protestant principle, 116 f.
Symbol, 59–63, 72, 74, 137; and
    ousia, 113; and person, 69; and
    reality, 60–61; and sign, 61, 68 f.;
    as the Other, 63; as paradoxical,
    68, 141; of God, 72; ontology
    of, 113 f., 140; Rahner on, 59;
    theology of, 66
Symbolizing, 113

Tanabe, Hajime, 72 f., 114
Tariki, 81; *see also* Jiriki
Tathata (suchness), 97
Temporality, 78
Temporalization, 45 f., 54
Tertullian, 58
Text, 134; nothing outside of, 11;
    reader's relation to, 121; voice of,
    121; sacred, 13
Theism, 75

Theology, 2, 30, 36; aphairetic, 28, 30; end of, 36; kataphatic, 30; mystical, 2, 47 f.; negative, 51 f., 108; of Paul and Reformers, 85 n. 2; of symbol, 137; symbolical, 2 f.; *see also* Negative theology

Theonomy, 81, 82, 115

Thinking, 101; ethical, 50, 135 f.; apocalyptic, 135; as thanking, 123; nonontological (an/ontological), 106, 135 f.; ontological, 50, 135; openness of, 123

Thomas Aquinas, 23 n. 7

Tillich, Paul, 72 f., 87, 94; and Buddhism, 87; and history of religions, 87; between orthodoxy and secularism, 87; compared with Nishitani, 73; on nonbeing, 7; on secularity, 93

Time, 54, 76

Totaliter aliter, 6; *see also* Otherness

Totality, 31, 44

Trace, 24 n. 28, 135

Transcendence, 144 f.; and excendence, 50; metaphysical, 50

Trinity, 69, 109 f., 114, 139 f.; absurdity of, 141; community in, 64; Origen on, 58; problems in

conception of, 110–12; roots of, 113, 137 f.

Typology, 88 f., 94, 97

U (being), 142

Ultimate concern, 80

Ultimate reality, 147 f.; and daily life, 94

Undecidability, 21

Understanding, 74; the "as"-structure of, 23 n. 12

Via negativa, 11

Virtual, and actual, 45

Vocative, 106

Void, 32

Weil, Simone, 42

White, as absence of light, 30

Whitehead, Alfred North, 82

Will, 17, 75–78; as *curvatus in se*, 77 f.; autonomous, 77

Withdrawal, 127, 129

Wondrous Being, 148

Word, deconstruction of, 15

Writing, 121, 136

Zange, 82

Zen, 73